The

GREATEST WAR STORIES NEVER TOLD

ALSO BY RICK BEYER

The Greatest Stories Never Told

Collins

An Imprint of HarperCollins*Publishers*

HISTORY. *Presents*

The

GREATEST WAR STORIES NEVER TOLD

100 *Tales from Military History to Astonish,*
Bewilder, & *Stupefy*

by Rick Beyer

THE GREATEST WAR STORIES NEVER TOLD. Copyright © 2005 by A&E Television Networks. All rights reserved. Printed in the United States of America. No part of this book may be used or reproduced in any manner whatsoever without written permission except in the case of brief quotations embodied in critical articles and reviews. For information, address HarperCollins Publishers, 195 Broadway, New York, NY 10007.

HarperCollins books may be purchased for educational, business, or sales promotional use. For information, please e-mail the Special Markets Department at SPsales@harpercollins.com.

Book design based on design by Judith Stagnitto Abbate/Abbate Design
Book layout by Renato Stanisic

Library of Congress Cataloging-in-Publication Data

Beyer, Rick, 1956–
   The greatest war stories never told: 100 tales from military history to astonish, bewilder, and stupefy/by Rick Beyer —1st ed.
      p. cm
   Includes bibliographical references.
   ISBN-10: 0-06-076017-6
   ISBN-13: 978-0-06-076017-5
   1. Military history—Anecdotes. I. Title.

D25.5.B45   2005
355'.009—dc22   2005045517

      18 19 20 ❖/RRD 30 29 28 27 26 25 24 23

for Marilyn

"War is hell," said William Tecumseh Sherman. But it has also spawned some mind-bending true stories.

Consider: a topless dancer saved the Roman Empire, and Daniel Boone was once tried for treason. One conflict broke out because of a soccer game while another was halted so a soccer game could be played. An African-American unit managed to serve on both sides during the Civil War. And Santa Anna, the general who massacred the defenders of the Alamo, was instrumental in the invention of modern chewing gum.

I am a lifelong history enthusiast lucky enough to be earning a living doing what I love: making history documentaries. A few years ago I got the chance to produce a series of history minutes for THE HISTORY CHANNEL.® The *Timelab 2000*® series, hosted by Sam Waterston, was so well received that it led to my first book, *The Greatest Stories Never Told*. I filled that book with the kind of history I love—stories that turn your expectations upside down and leave you shaking your head in wonderment. Happily, readers and critics enjoyed the stories as much as I did.

Now I have turned my attention to the subject of war and warriors, human experience at its most concentrated and extreme. For better or worse, war has been a fundamental part of history, touching every generation and reaching into every corner of the globe. "War means fighting," said Confederate general Nathan Bedford Forrest, "and fighting means killing." Hard words, and true. But there is more to war than death and destruction. War can be a catalyst for change, an engine for innovation, and an arena for valor, deceit, intrigue, ambition, audacity, folly, and, yes, humor. That's what makes military history so compelling.

Beyond the big-name battles and celebrated soldiers lies a wealth of amazing characters and unbelievable happenings. As I did for my first book, I set out on a quest for the unusual, the surprising, and the ironic—stories that cry out to be told. Here they are in your hand, gathered from more than two thousand years of history. The very first one is about an elite military unit composed entirely of gay soldiers, and the last is about Pentagon pizza deliveries predicting the start of the first Gulf War. In between you can find out why George Washington's house was named after the inventor of grog, what the Mafia did to help win World War II, and how a Civil War general who didn't know a note of music still managed to write a song that everybody knows.

Though I have read a fair bit of history, I was quite amazed by some of the stories I came across. Each of them has been painstakingly researched and carefully fact-checked. Many a fascinating tale has failed to make the cut because it didn't hold up under scrutiny. The ones that made it in, bizarre as they might seem, are as true as I know how to make them.

"It is well that war is so terrible," blurted out Robert E. Lee in the midst of a battle, "or we should grow to love it." Human beings have been fascinated by war since the dawn of history. What could be more dramatic, after all, than high-stakes, life-and-death conflict on a grand scale? For all of war's horrors, its pull remains strong. I hope that the stories that follow truly do "astonish, bewilder, and stupefy." I also hope they will prompt readers to ponder the ultimate folly of war, and why it is that we never quite manage to make it a thing of the past.

The

GREATEST WAR STORIES NEVER TOLD

THE SACRED BAND

An elite fighting unit like no other.

The Spartans of ancient Greece were among the most famous and fearsome warriors of all time. Never have there been a people more single-mindedly devoted to the military arts. Spartan boys were taken from home to attend military school at age seven, and every male between twenty and sixty had to serve in the armed forces. The result was that Sparta fielded the most powerful military force in Greece.

Nevertheless, the vaunted Spartan army was defeated by Thebes at the battle of Leuctra in 371 B.C. The turning point in the battle came when an elite Theban military unit known as the Sacred Band led a breakthrough against the Spartan right wing. Famed for both its fighting ability and its unusual makeup, the Sacred Band consisted of 300 soldiers who all had something in common.

They were gay.

This one-of-a-kind unit consisted of 150 homosexual couples. The idea was that every man would be motivated to fight to his maximum ability both to protect his lover *and* to avoid shaming himself in front of his lover. In modern military jargon, it was thought that this Theban "band of lovers" would enjoy a high degree of unit cohesion.

And it worked. The Sacred Band stood undefeated for more than thirty years. When it was finally overcome in battle against Macedonians, it is said that the unit was so unwilling to yield that every single man fought to the death.

> ## "PERISH ANY MAN WHO SUSPECTS THAT THESE MEN EITHER DID OR SUFFERED ANYTHING THAT WAS BASE."

–PHILIP II OF MACEDON,
VIEWING THE BODIES OF
THE SACRED BAND SLAIN
IN BATTLE BY HIS ARMY

The Spartans were the original men of few words. Sparta was part of a larger area known as Laconia, which is where the word "laconic" comes from. The story is told that Philip II sent a threatening message to the Spartans, warning, "If I enter Laconia, I will level it to the ground." The Spartans' one-word reply: "If . . ."

The Spartans' daily regimen was so demanding that Plutarch claimed they were the only men in the world for whom war was a welcome rest from training.

ARCHIMEDES' SECRET WEAPON

How one old man held off an entire Roman fleet.

In 213 B.C., a Roman fleet under the command of Marcus Claudius Marcellus attacked the Greek city-state of Syracuse. Marcellus was confident he could take Syracuse in five days. Instead, it took more than a year, thanks to the ingenuity of one old man.

Archimedes.

Archimedes is best remembered for shouting "Eureka!" in his bath and running through the streets naked. But there was much more to the man than that. He was Einstein and Edison combined, the greatest scientist of the ancient world, and also a brilliant inventor. As the military adviser to the king of Syracuse, he spent years devising mysterious "engines" to protect the city. When the Romans came, Syracuse put Archimedes' machines to work.

There were large catapults capable of hurling rocks the size of wagons, and small catapults called "scorpions" that shot darts at the Romans. A giant grappling claw lifted Roman ships by the bow and smashed them against the rocks. Mousetrap-like mechanisms levered giant weights down upon Roman siege ladders.

Then there were the mirrors.

Archimedes, according to several chroniclers, created a series of mirrors that could focus the sun's energy on ships and cause them to burst into flame—a death ray in the ancient world.

Marcellus had to admit he could not take the city by storm. He was forced to lay siege to it for many months before he finally found a way in. Archimedes was killed in the sack of the city, but not before demonstrating that the genius of one man could prove equal to all the military might in Rome.

Archimedes so terrorized Roman sailors that every time they spied a rope or a piece of wood sticking out from the walls of Syracuse, they feared it was another of his fearsome engines, and fled. "The Romans" said Plutarch, "began to think they were fighting with the gods."

> ## ARCHIMEDES USES MY SHIPS TO LADLE SEAWATER INTO HIS WINE CUPS.
>
> —ROMAN GENERAL MARCUS CLAUDIUS MARCELLUS

Numerous historians have expressed skepticism about the mirrors. But in 1747, French scientist George-Louis Leclerc de Buffon pulled off a successful demonstration of the technique. He used an array of mirrors to make a piece of wood two hundred feet away burst into flame. It was a great PR stunt that made him famous across Europe.

UP AGAINST THE WALL

Hail Caesar and the bold tactics that led to his greatest victory.

Julius Caesar had just suffered his first defeat in six years as a proconsul. The tribes of Gaul, united at last, were threatening his demise. A long way from Rome, he was short on food, and had no hope of reinforcements.

This was the prologue for one of the most boldly conceived battles in military history.

When Caesar came upon an army of eighty thousand Gauls holed up in the fortified town of Alesia, he ordered his legions to build a siege wall encircling the town. Then Caesar learned that another army of two hundred thousand Gauls was coming to crush his army and lift the siege. What to do?

Caesar's solution was as daring as it was innovative. He ordered his legions to build a *second* set of fortifications around the city. While the first wall faced inward, *this* one faced outward, encircling his army and protecting it from the outside.

Military history records nothing else like it. Caesar had surrounded an army larger than his own, and then found himself surrounded by a second, still larger army. When the Gauls attacked, the Roman forces between the two walls found themselves fighting in both directions, against armies that outnumbered them six to one.

Impossible as it seems, Caesar won this battle, personally leading his reserve force out of the fortifications to attack at a critical moment. He defeated the army surrounding him, forcing the surrender of Alesia and the army within.

That decisive victory brought peace to Gaul. Caesar's reputation, already glittering, soared to new heights. And an emperor's throne awaited.

The double siege walls built by Caesar's army were one of the greatest military engineering feats in history. These reconstructed fortifications show the complexity of the walls, complete with earthworks, trenches filled with sharpened stakes, wooden guard towers, and palisade walls. Remarkably, the Romans completed the two sets of fortifications in little over a month.

The captured soldiers inside the town became the slaves of the soldiers who had defeated them. They were lucky. After conquering one rebellious town, Caesar ordered that everyone who had borne arms against him should have their hands chopped off, as a warning to others. Caesar's eight-year conquest of Gaul made him rich, famous, and powerful, but the province paid a high price: a million dead, a million more enslaved, and eight hundred towns taken by storm.

The inner and outer lines of Caesar's fortifications were about two hundred yards apart at their closest point, nearly a thousand yards apart at their widest.

WARRIOR PRINCESS

She took on the armies of Rome . . . and almost beat them.

Hell hath no fury like a woman scorned. And Queen Boudicca had been worse than scorned by the Romans. After the death of her husband, who was king of a Celtic tribe known as the Iceni, Roman authorities moved in to annex his kingdom, plunder his property, and humiliate his family. When Boudicca dared to protest, she was flogged and her daughters were raped.

The Romans soon discovered the error of their ways.

Boudicca vowed vengeance, and raised a huge army of Celts to expel the Roman oppressors. She attacked a Roman colony at Colchester, slaughtering its residents and putting it to the torch. Informed that the Roman Ninth Legion was rushing to the colony's aid, she laid an ambush and annihilated 1,500 elite Roman infantryman.

When the Roman governor heard she was marching on London, he and his forces abandoned the city. A prudent move. Boudicca's angry army murdered and mutilated everyone they found there, and burned London to the ground.

The Romans were terrified of Boudicca. Though no strangers to the brutality of war themselves, her blood lust astounded them. "The British could not wait to cut throats, hang, burn, and crucify," wrote Roman historian Tacitus, who estimated that her army killed seventy thousand Roman soldiers and civilians.

Eventually the Romans scraped together an army to meet

Boudicca in battle, and defeated the Celts. Tens of thousands of Boudicca's soldiers were slaughtered, and she chose to take poison rather than be captured.

Rome would rule Britain for three more centuries . . . but they never forgot the warrior woman who almost voted them off the island.

> **SHE WAS VERY TALL, IN APPEARANCE MOST TERRIFYING, IN THE GLANCE OF HER EYE MOST FIERCE . . . A GREAT MASS OF THE TAWNIEST HAIR FELL TO HER HIPS.**
>
> —ROMAN HISTORIAN DIO CASSIUS, DESCRIBING BOUDICCA

Boudicca's torching of London left an indelible mark on the city that remains to this day. Archaeologists digging down through the strata have found a layer of ash three feet thick from the time of the fire that testifies to the total destruction she wreaked upon the city.

DARING DANCER

The circus girl who saved an empire.

Theodora was a striptease dancer with one heck of an act. Crowds flocked to the circus in Constantinople to watch her dance half-naked with lions. One of those who found himself mesmerized by Theodora was Justinian, nephew of the emperor and next in line to rule the Byzantine Empire. He fell in love with the beautiful Theodora and married her. When Justinian eventually became emperor, Theodora became his empress.

Lucky for him—because her fearlessness would one day save his empire.

A few years into Justinian's reign, a tax revolt broke out. There was chaos and rioting in the streets. It seemed the end of Justinian's reign might be at hand. Shaken, the emperor prepared to flee. A ship was ordered to stand by, ready at any moment to take him and his wife into exile.

But Theodora wouldn't have it. The one time circus girl made it clear she would rather die than surrender the royal rank she had attained. "Royalty is a good burial shroud," Theodora calmly told her husband.

Her words filled Justinian with new resolve. Instead of fleeing, he sent out his imperial guard to fight the rebels, who were eventually crushed.

Justinian and Theodora reigned together for another twenty-one years, and Justinian for seventeen more years after her death.

Famed nineteenth-century actress Sarah Bernhardt as Theodora.

Men of senatorial rank were forbidden to marry actresses and dancers, who were considered little better than prostitutes. Justinian had to convince his uncle, the emperor, to repeal that law so he could marry Theodora.

AN ISLAMIC EUROPE?

Imagine Notre Dame Cathedral as a mosque. It could have happened but for one pivotal battle.

In the year 610, the angel Gabriel came to the Prophet Muhammad in a dream. Thus was Islam born, and it soon spread like wildfire. By the year 732, just one hundred years after Muhammad's death, an Arab empire with thirty million Muslim subjects stretched from India all the way to Spain. It seemed only a matter of time before all of Europe fell under Islam's sway.

Some of the most ardent converts were nomadic Moors in North Africa. They were determined to spread the word with their swords. In 732, a mighty army of eighty thousand Moors roared through Spain, crossed the Pyrenees Mountains, and rode into what is now France. "Everything gave way to their scimitars," wrote one Arab chronicler. The Moors swept away everything in their path, and came within a hundred miles of Paris.

But fate intervened in the form of Charles, king of the Franks. He led his army south from Paris and met the Moors near the town of Tours. In a desperate battle, his foot soldiers beat off attack after attack from the Moorish horsemen, and finally routed the enemy.

The Battle of Tours may have been one of the most important in history. Had the Moors been victorious there, much of Europe might have been dominated by Islam instead of Christianity . . . and the world would be a very different place.

The battle earned King Charles a ferocious nickname. Henceforth he became known as Charles Martel, in English, Charles the Hammer.

" **THE TWO GREAT HOSTS OF THE TWO LANGUAGES AND THE TWO CREEDS WERE SET IN ARRAY AGAINST EACH OTHER.** "

—AN ARAB CHRONICLER OF THE BATTLE

SPOILS OF WAR

How an Islamic invasion led to one of the world's wonders.

An army of Arabs, Berbers, and Spanish Moors invaded Sicily in 832. They were known to Europeans as the Saracens. Within fifty years they had taken over most of the island, and they ruled it in the name of Islam for two centuries.

In 1004 the Saracens sacked the Italian city-state of Pisa. The citizens there thought of themselves as traders, not fighters, but in response to Saracen attacks they built up a navy to defend themselves. Then they turned the tables on their one-time invaders, undertaking a daring raid on Palermo, the capital of Saracen Sicily. They ravaged the city, sinking many Saracen ships. Only one enemy vessel remained afloat, and it was used to bring back a shipload of plunder.

Back home, the powers that be decided that a portion of the booty should be used to fund the construction of a grand cathedral, which was duly built. A cathedral wouldn't be complete without a bell tower, and in 1172 a wealthy widow named

Berta Di Bernardo left "sixty coins" in her will for the construction of one. Work began immediately but kept getting interrupted by battles with Florence and other Italian city-states. It took almost two centuries to finish it.

Maybe that's where the problem began. Or maybe it would have happened anyway, what with the structure's shallow foundation and shifting subsoil. For of course the cathedral bell tower that the Pisans built had a flaw. A flaw that would one day be seen as it's greatest glory, and make it known around the world.

From an Islamic invasion and a widow's will: the Leaning Tower of Pisa.

The tower wasn't even finished in 1298 when the first commission was formed to look into its stability. Seventeen such commissions have been formed over the centuries, some helping, some hurting. Scientists believe that the most recent commission's efforts have stabilized the tower for the next few hundred years.

In the summer of 1944, the fate of the tower was in the hands of U.S. Army sergeant Leon Weckstein. The Germans were thought to be using the tower as an observation post. Weckstein was sent forward with orders to call in an artillery barrage if he saw any movement in it. "Had I seen the glitter of one shiny button, even for a second, the tower would have become a pile of gravel," he said later. Seeing nothing suspicious, however, Weckstein held off giving the order for the tower's destruction. Eventually, Allied generals decided to spare the landmark.

HISTORY'S HITMEN

The group that may have been the world's first terrorists.

During the eleventh century, a rebellious Islamic sect took command of a mountaintop castle outside of Teheran. They set about trying to win converts, and soon held a chain of castles across the Middle East.

This breakaway group of radical Shiites waged war against the rulers of the Islamic world, chiefly through acts of terrorism and "hits" carried out on political leaders. Their weapon of choice was the dagger, and they murdered princes, scholars, crusaders, and caliphs—whoever were their enemies of the moment.

In many ways, they were the Al-Qaeda of their day. Their specialty was dramatic, high-profile killings—sometimes for the purpose of advancing their agenda, other times to raise money. Members of the group believed that the murders they carried out would earn them immediate and eternal bliss.

For more than 150 years they held sway. In the 1200s, Mongol warriors, led by Genghis Khan's grandson, Hulagu, captured their mountain strongholds, and their reign of terror was over.

Crusaders brought tales of this faction back to Europe. Their very name evoked shivers of terror, and it is still remembered today. Whenever a political leader is murdered, it evokes the memory of this ancient cult whose methods seem all too modern.

The Assassins.

The word "assassin" is actually a corruption of the group's original name, the Hashishi. Crusaders wrongly thought that meant the terrorists were hashish eaters, which added to their fearsome reputation. Other stories, mostly myths, also circulated about the sect. One told of how their leader ordered two followers to jump off a tower to their deaths simply to demonstrate to some visitors from the West the total authority he held over his men.

The founder of the Assassins was Hassan-I-Sabbah. Among those he ordered executed were both of his sons, one for drinking wine. His sect could be flexible in its allegiances. They executed Crusader leaders, but also carried out execution attempts on behalf of the Crusaders when it suited them.

The ruins of an Assassin castle in Syria. It was a virtually impregnable fortress with three layers of defensive walls.

THE SWALLOWS OF VOLOHAI

How did cat whiskers and bird wings help Genghis Kahn conquer an empire?

Genghis Khan was a brilliant military leader who united the Mongol tribes and created a fearsome army with himself at its head. In 1207 his men swept across the Gobi Desert and began to attack China. But they were halted at the walled city of Volohai, their dreams of conquest stalled. Here the hard-riding Mongols discovered that their cavalry tactics were virtually useless in attacking a heavily fortified city.

It was time for some outside-the-box thinking, and the great Khan was up to the challenge. He offered to end the siege in exchange for an unusual tribute: one thousand cats and ten thousand swallows. One can imagine the puzzlement of the town's defenders upon receiving this message, but they decided to comply.

Wrong decision.

When they delivered the tribute, Kahn ordered his men to tie puffs of cotton to the animals' tails, and then set the cotton on fire. The frightened creatures fled back to their city. A thousand fires seemed to break out everywhere at the same time, and the citizens of Volohai rushed to fight them.

At that moment, the Mongols attacked!

Volohai fell. And though it would take decades, all of China would follow.

His experience at Volohai persuaded Genghis Khan to adopt some of his enemy's tactics. He began to use siege engines—catapults, towers, and explosives—manned by captured Chinese engineers. These gave his army the ability to attack the fortified walls of Chinese cities.

Another strategy of Khan was to march newly captured locals at the front of his ranks. Inhabitants of the area under attack would be hesitant to hurt their neighbors, shielding the Mongols until they got close enough to attack.

DIVINE WIND

The storm that saved Japan.

This was war on an unprecedented scale. Kublai Khan had already completed the conquest of China begun by his grandfather, Genghis Khan. Now he had assembled 140,000 warriors to invade the Japanese islands. A fleet of nine thousand ships carried them to Japan. It seemed that nothing could stop them from defeating Japan and absorbing it into the Mongol Empire.

But everything changed when the winds suddenly rose with a fury and a powerful typhoon slammed into the Japanese coast, wreaking havoc on the invasion force. Ships were dashed upon the rocks. Thousands drowned. Chinese warriors who managed to stagger ashore were easy prey for the Japanese, who slaughtered them at will. It is thought that as many as 100,000 of the invaders perished.

Japan was saved. The Japanese people gave credit to the gods, calling the typhoon that wrecked the invasion force "The Divine Wind."

It was a name that would become familiar in another war centuries later, when it would be adopted by Japanese warriors willing to sacrifice their own lives in a last-ditch bid to turn defeat into victory. They too referred to themselves as "The Divine Wind." Or in Japanese:

Kamikaze.

This was actually the second time Kublai Khan tried to invade Japan. The first time, seven years before, a smaller invasion force was also stymied by a typhoon that scattered or sunk much of the invasion fleet.

A kamikaze plane attacking the USS Missouri in April of 1945. It hit the Missouri a glancing blow moments after Seaman Len Schmidt snapped this picture, but no one on the ship was hurt. During the last year of World War II, suicide planes sunk 34 U.S. ships and damaged 288. More than four thousand Japanese pilots sacrificed their lives in kamikaze missions.

ARMS RACE

One story that may well be a load of manure.

It began as a "fire drug" developed by Chinese alchemists. It eventually exploded into a fuel for killing that is now nearly a thousand years old.

Gunpowder.

The first known Chinese recipe for gunpowder dates back to 1044. Cannons appeared in China a century or so later, but gun technology didn't really take off until the weapons made their way to Europe some two hundred years after that. It didn't take long for the Europeans to turn primitive "bombards," as early cannons were known, into wonder-weapons that helped them extend their power over much of the globe.

iu nel anno MD XXXII. effendo per Prefetto in Verona il Magnifid
r Leonardo Iuftiniano. V n capo de bombardieri amiciffimo di quel noftro ami
ene in concorrentia con un altro (al prefente capo de bombardieri in Padoa
giorno accadete che fra loro fu propofto il medemo che a noi propoffe que

If the Chinese had cannons first, how was it that the Europeans won that early arms race?

The most effective gunpowder is about three-quarters saltpeter, mixed with charcoal and sulfur. And the most common source for saltpeter then was animal dung. But the Chinese had fewer domesticated animals than the Europeans, so saltpeter was harder to come by in China. Made with less saltpeter, Chinese gunpowder was less powerful.

Being comparatively richer in farm animals, and thus saltpeter, the Europeans were able to make more potent gunpowder, which paved the way for better and more effective weapons.

And that's no bull.

The picture below is the first known representation of a European firearm, found in a 1326 manuscript. Guns such as these were employed in 1331 at the siege of Civalde, in Italy, the earliest known use of cannons in a European battle.

Once cannons were introduced to Europe, every prince wanted his own. But cannons were expensive, and cash in short supply. Then silver was discovered in the mountains of what is now the Czech Republic, near the town of Joachimsthal. The millions of coins minted there were known as thalers—or, as they came to be called in English, "dollars." The new currency helped make gun manufacturing a growth industry.

During the 1300s, Chinese engineers focused their energies not so much on guns as on bombs. These were launched by catapults and given fantastic names such as "Dropping from Heaven Bomb," and "Bandit Burning Vision-Confusing Magic Fire-ball."

"A CHILD'S TOY OF SOUND AND FIRE."

—ROGER BACON IN 1267, THE EARLIEST KNOWN EUROPEAN REFERENCE TO GUNPOWDER

DANGEROUS GAMES

*A trip back to the day
when soccer and
golf were a threat to
national security.*

In 1314, England's King Edward II issued a royal edict banning the game of soccer. It wasn't because he was morally opposed to the game but because he believed that it's very popularity was a threat to his realm. He decreed harsh prison terms for anyone found playing.

Other British kings followed suit. Edward III, Richard II, and Henry IV issued their own bans. In 1457, King James II of Scotland banned soccer *and* golf. In 1491, Scottish king James IV issued this decree: "It is statute and ordained that in no place of the Realme there be used Fute-ball, Golf, or uther unprofitable sports."

So what was it about soccer and golf and "uther" sports that was such a huge threat? The kings considered these activities "unprofitable" because they were distracting men from archery practice, which was essential to the defense of their countries. Without a populace of trained archers, neither England nor Scotland could raise effective armies in times of crisis.

But kings' edicts ultimately proved no match for men's passion for sport. The laws were ignored and eventually forgotten. Soccer and golf continued to thrive, despite the kings who saw them as a national-security nightmare.

> ## WE COMMAND AND FORBID ON BEHALF OF THE KING, ON PAIN OF IMPRISONMENT, SUCH GAMES TO BE USED.
>
> —EDWARD II, BANNING SOCCER IN 1314

Not all royalty was down on golf. Mary Queen of Scots was an avid golfer. She paid a price for it in 1563, when she was castigated for taking to the links shortly after the murder of her husband (in which she may have had a hand).

GOD IS IN THE DETAILS

Joan of Arc's name is so familiar that we forget how amazing her story really was.

J oan of Arc was just a seventeen-year-old peasant girl when she led a French army to a momentous victory against the English at Orleans in 1428.

Joan had been hearing voices since the age of thirteen, and they told her that God wanted her to help Charles, the Dauphin (heir to the French throne), defeat the English and be crowned king. What she did to make that happen—in a time when women were regarded as property—beggars the imagination.

1. She talked her uncle into taking her to the local military commander.
2. She convinced the commander to provide a military escort to take her to the Dauphin.
3. She convinced a group of priests that God was really speaking to her, and that she should be allowed to meet with the Dauphin.
4. In less than five minutes she convinced Charles to give her an army.
5. She persuaded grizzled veterans of the war against England that they should take orders from a seventeen-year-old girl. Further, she got them to give up cursing and sex while serving under her.
6. In an age when war meant hand-to-hand combat, even for commanders, Joan survived numerous battles while never wielding a weapon.
7. Not only did she lead her army to victory at Orleans, she also liberated dozens of French towns and defeated another British army at Patay.

Was Joan actually inspired by God? Her soldiers thought so, and so did the Catholic Church, which made her a saint. If divine inspiration didn't actually play a role, Joan certainly had amazing powers of persuasion and one hell of a run of luck.

> ## HERE BEGIN THE PROCEEDINGS IN MATTER OF FAITH AGAINST A DEAD WOMAN, JEANNE, COMMONLY KNOWN AS THE MAID.

—THE OPENING WORDS FROM THE RECORD OF
JOAN OF ARC'S HERESY TRIAL

Captured by opposition French forces and handed over to the British, Joan was tried for heresy. The trial was rigged and the verdict certain, though the prosecution could not produce a single witness to speak against her. Nonetheless, she was burned at the stake on May 30, 1431.

WEAPONS WIZARD

The machinations of a military maestro.

Leonardo da Vinci was a painter, a sculptor, a scientist, and an engineer. He was also a one-man military industrial complex. Although he described himself as a pacifist, and called war "the most bestial madness," da Vinci had a lifelong fascination with all things military. He designed an astonishing number of weapons and combat devices, many of them centuries ahead of their time.

In his notebooks can be found designs for a self-propelled armored tank, a giant mechanical crossbow, a machine gun, and a helicopter. He sketched out a grenade with tail fins to be launched by a bowman, and a prefabricated portable bridge that armies could use to cross small steams. Da Vinci even designed a steam-powered cannon, which he claimed could fire a sixty-pound ball a distance of two-thirds of a mile.

While many of Leonardo's ideas never got off the drawing board, others proved highly practical. During his career da Vinci served as a military engineer to several European warlords, including the notorious Cesare Borgia. He designed fortifications so advanced that nothing like them was seen again for centuries. He created mortars that rained down a shower of stones on enemy heads.

Had da Vinci pushed his concepts harder, he might have dramatically changed the face of Renaissance warfare. But he was notorious for leaving a project unfinished and moving on to the next grand idea.

Leonardo is best known today as the artistic giant who painted the enigmatic *Mona Lisa*. But it may be in the *military* arts that his genius showed through the most.

The tank that Leonardo designed was armored with heavy wooden beams and propelled by men inside operating hand cranks. It was designed to make quick penetrations into enemy lines that could be followed up by infantry . . . which is exactly how motor-driven tanks were first used more than four centuries later in World War I.

> **WHATEVER THE SITUATION, I CAN INVENT AN INFINITE VARIETY OF MACHINES FOR BOTH ATTACK AND DEFENSE.**

—LEONARDO DA VINCI, IN A LETTER TO THE DUKE OF MILAN

When the leaders of Florence sought da Vinci's advice in attacking Pisa, he came up with a scheme to divert the river Arno, which would deprive the Pisans of water and cut off their access to the harbor. Breathtaking in conception, it was, like many of da Vinci's ideas, too difficult to execute. The effort was ultimately abandoned.

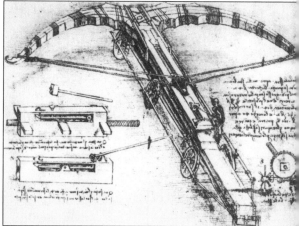

SIEGE OF BREAD AND BUTTER

A famous scientist, a tasty spread, and a wartime outbreak of disease.

To Polish astronomer Nicolas Copernicus we owe our understanding that the earth moves around the sun, not the sun around the earth. It was a discovery that revolutionized science. Do we also owe to him the custom of putting butter on our bread?

In 1519, Copernicus was called upon to command Polish forces besieged in the fortified town of Allenstein, a Polish town on the Prussian border.

During the siege, the town was struck by plague. Copernicus isolated the town's bread as being the source of the disease. But he suspected that it wasn't the bread itself, rather the fact that something was contaminating it. Sanitary conditions in the beleaguered town were marginal at best, and the coarse black loaves could be dropped in the dirty streets, or otherwise contaminated, without even showing it.

That's when a fellow by the name of Gerhard Glickselig suggested to Copernicus that the bread loaves be covered with a thin layer of light-colored spread. That would make it obvious if the bread was dropped or if debris fell on it, and people could avoid eating it. Copernicus ordered it be done, and the plague soon ended.

Thus were married bread and butter, at least for the first time that we know of. It didn't become common in Europe until the following century. And so we honor Copernicus as a man ahead of his time in matters of cuisine as well as the cosmos.

True to form, Copernicus employed the scientific method to discover the source of the disease. He divided the town's residents into four groups and fed them different things. The group that got no bread was the only one that remained plague free.

Copernicus's revolution-
ary theory about the
earth revolving around
the sun was published
on his deathbed, sparing
him conflict with the
Vatican, which would
plague Galileo and oth-
ers who followed in his
footsteps.

NICOLAI CO
PERNICI TORINENSIS
DE REVOLUTIONIBUS ORBI-
um cœlestium, Libri VI.

Habes in hoc opere iam recens nato, & ædito,
studiose lector, Motus stellarum, tam fixarum,
quàm erraticarum, cum ex ueteribus, tum etiam
ex recentibus observationibus restitutos: & no-
uis insuper ac admirabilibus hypothesibus or-
natos. Habes etiam Tabulas expeditissimas, ex
quibus eosdem ad quoduis tempus quàm facilli
me calculare poteris. Igitur eme, lege, fruere.

ἀγεωμέτρητος ὀυδεὶς ἐισίτω.

Norimbergæ apud Ioh. Petreium,
Anno M. D. XLIII.

Allenstein was being besieged by the Teutonic Knights, a religious order of German knights formed in Jerusalem during the
Crusades. Later they conquered Prussia, and battled with Polish
kings for centuries.

FIGHTING TURTLES

The most amazing warships you've never heard of.

The famous Civil War battle between Monitor and Merrimac in 1862 ushered in the age of ironclad warships. Or so it is generally assumed. In fact, a brilliant Korean admiral introduced the ironclad more than 250 years earlier.

Japanese invaders landed in Korea in 1592, and won several quick victories. The country was on the verge of defeat until Korean admiral Yi Sun-Sin stepped into the breach with a fleet of innovative vessels he had helped design. He called them *kobukson,* or "turtle ships." These were the world's first ironclads, the earliest ancestors of modern warships.

The turtle ships had rounded roofs covered with iron plating and spikes to ward off boarders. Ports cut into the side of the turtle ships could accommodate up to twenty-six cannons. The fearsome warships bore a remarkable resemblance to the Civil War ironclads that would see action centuries later, except that they were powered by oarsmen instead of steam engines.

The Japanese had many more ships than the Koreans, but they found that their guns could not penetrate the armor, and their fire arrows failed to set the turtle ships ablaze. A master tactician, Admiral Yi used the *kobukson* to win a series of battles against the larger Japanese fleet, enabling Korea to drive off the Japanese invaders. In 1598, during a second Japanese invasion, Yi achieved an even bigger victory, destroying more than two hundred Japanese ships.

Admiral Yi was killed in that battle, and his death spelled the death of the turtle ships. No one else had the vision to use them effectively, so the age of the ironclad warship would have to wait.

Some forty thousand Japanese sailors and soldiers were killed in Yi's last battle. That's more than twice the number of Spanish who died when England defeated the Armada in 1588.

There are no surviving turtle ships, or even the plans from one. This replica was built from a description contained in Admiral Yi's diaries. Smoke could be poured out of the dragon head, a tactic Admiral Yi used to confuse and frighten the Japanese—the first recorded use of a smoke screen in a naval battle.

Like Admiral Nelson centuries later, Yi was killed at his moment of supreme victory, about to win a battle that would save his homeland. His last words: "Do not weep, do not announce my death. Beat the drum, blow the trumpet, wave the flag for advance."

A FALLING-OUT IN PRAGUE

It might have been downright funny . . . if it hadn't started a war.

In May of 1618, three men were hurled out a high window of Hradcany Castle in Prague. Instead of being killed or badly hurt, they landed in a dung heap that cushioned their fall. They took to their heels and scampered off, their pride being the only thing seriously injured.

The event sounds almost comical, but it proved to have tragic results.

The men were official representatives of the Roman Catholic Hapsburg emperor. An enraged crowd of Protestant nobles had thrown them out the window to protest the closing of several protestant churches. This act of rebellion outraged the emperor, and triggered a war.

It began as a struggle between Catholics and Protestants in Bohemia. Soon Austria got involved, then Denmark and Sweden. Shortly thereafter, Poland, France, and the Netherlands joined in. The scandal in Bohemia had exploded into a seemingly endless conflict that engulfed much of Europe: the Thirty Years' War.

Ten million people would die in the war, more than a quarter of the population of Central Europe. When it was over, the authority of the Roman Catholic Church was dealt a major blow. What emerged from the war was a Europe filled with sovereign states that could choose their own religions . . . the Europe we still know today.

The incident became known as the "Defenestration of Prague"—defenestration being a fancy word for throwing someone out the window. It has a history in Prague. Two hundred years before this defenestration, several town councillors were thrown out the window of Prague City Hall, an event that sparked a war of its own.

The men were thrown out of the middle set of windows. The monument below marks where they landed. They claimed the Virgin Mary had magically appeared to cushion their fall, but onlookers said it was manure piled up in what was at that time the castle moat.

When a peace conference was finally called to end the war, it required six months of negotiations just to agree on where everyone would sit. After another year of discussions, the Treaty of Westphalia was signed.

DREBBEL'S DREAM

The forgotten vessel that was the first of its kind.

Not long after the Pilgrims set sail from England aboard the *Mayflower*, a far different vessel ventured forth on a journey up London's Thames River. It traveled only a few miles, but it did something the *Mayflower* did not do, and could not do.

It traveled underwater.

The vessel, designed by Dutch inventor Cornelius Drebbel, was the first successful submarine ever built. Drebbel had been hired as a court inventor for England's King James and was trying to convince the Royal Navy that this was the vessel of the future.

Drebbel took a fishing boat and built a wooden roof over it. Then he covered the whole thing with greased leather. It was powered by twelve oarsmen, who breathed air that came through a snorkel tube. A sloping foredeck acted as a diving plane, and the vessel moved up the river about twelve feet underwater. Observers said it traveled from Westminster Palace to Greenwich, a distance of about four miles, in three hours.

The successful test of the boat piqued the king's interest, and Drebbel built two larger versions of his submarine. It is said that the king even took a ride in one of them. But the Royal Navy never did cotton to the contraption. They just couldn't imagine that a vessel that traveled underwater could have any military use. It would be nearly three centuries before they changed their minds.

Drebbel was a jack of all trades: glassmaker, engraver, alchemist, doctor, and, of course, inventor. Despite his many skills, he died in poverty in 1634.

The first submarine employed for military purposes was the Turtle, designed by David Bushnell of Connecticut. The one-man sub tried to attach a mine to a British man-of-war in New York Harbor in 1776. The effort failed and the mine exploded harmlessly. Wrote George Washington later: "I thought, and still think, that it was an effort of genius."

> **A CONCEIT OF THAT DESERVEDLY FAMOUS MECHANICIAN AND CHYMIST CORNELIUS DREBBEL.**

—DESCRIPTION OF DREBBEL'S BOAT BY SIR ROBERT BOYLE IN 1662

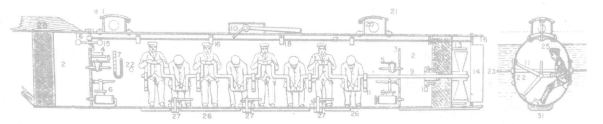

The first submarine successfully used in battle was the Hunley, a Confederate submarine that rammed the USS Housatonic with an explosive torpedo in 1864. The explosion sank the Housatonic but also sent the Hunley to the bottom off the coast of Charleston, South Carolina, costing the lives of everyone aboard.

BEES IN BATTLE

Battlefields have been abuzz with bees from ancient times till today.

In the closing stages of the Thirty Years' War, a Swedish army assaulted Kissengen, a walled city in Bavaria. The desperate defenders responded by throwing beehives off the wall into the ranks of the Swedes, who were forced to retreat in the face of stinging attacks from the angry swarm that enveloped them.

This was hardly unprecedented. When faced with the question "To bee or not to bee?" armies throughout the ages have consistently answered in the affirmative. The Romans frequently loaded their catapults with beehives and launched them upon their enemies. King Richard the Lionhearted did the same thing against the Saracens during the Crusades. The Saxons, the Moors, and the Hungarians also used them in various battles.

Bees have been used at sea as well. There is at least one recorded instance of sailors on a small ship in the Mediterranean climbing the rigging and throwing beehives down onto the deck of an attacking galley, instantly turning the tables on the larger ship.

Bee warfare hasn't gone out of style, either. Both sides in Vietnam created fearsome booby traps using hives of Asian honeybees, larger and more ferocious than their Western cousins. And at the dawn of the twenty-first century, Pentagon scientists are trying to recruit bees into the war on terror, training them to sniff out explosives. They hope the bees will be able to uncover landmines and bomb factories.

That would be a honey of a trick.

Bees may look fierce, but the truth is that they tend to respond only when provoked. Hives handled with care could be transported or loaded on a catapult with little problem. Once dashed against a wall or on the ground, however, their peace-loving populations turn into winged warriors seeking venomed vengeance.

I n the so-called Battle of the Bees during World War I, both British and German forces fighting for the East African city of Tanga were tormented by swarms of angry bees provoked by machine-gun fire disturbing their nests. Some soldiers were stung hundreds of times. During the Battle of Antietam in the Civil War, the 132nd Pennsylvania Infantry was routed by bees after Confederate shells broke open a nearby farmer's beehives.

The Romans made such frequent use of beehives in their catapults that some historians feel it contributed to a massive decline in the European bee population during the later stages of the Roman Empire.

THE SIEGE THAT GAVE BIRTH TO THE CROISSANT

An invading Turkish army provides the inspiration for a breakfast delicacy.

The croissant is not French—it was first baked in Austria. And its shape is anything but an accident. The popular pastry dates back to 1683. In that year an army of more than one hundred thousand Ottoman Turks was besieging the city of Vienna. They surrounded it for months, and residents inside the stout walls began to wonder if each day would be their last.

When the Turks tried tunneling under the walls, bakers working through the night heard the digging sounds and raised the alarm. This early warning prevented the Turks from breaching Vienna's walls, and helped save the city. Eventually an army under Poland's King John III reached Vienna and drove the Turks away.

The bakers celebrated the end of the siege in a remarkable way. They copied the crescent moon from their enemy's flag, and turned it into a commemorative pastry. It was called a *Kipfel* (German for "crescent") and it honored a victory that might never have happened but for the bakers themselves.

The Siege of Vienna is also believed by many to be the birthplace of the bagel. King John of Poland was widely known as a skilled horseman, and a baker supposedly created a roll in the shape of a stirrup to honor him. The Austrian word for stirrup is Bügel—eventually Americanized to "bagel." Can it be true that one battle did so much for so many breakfasts?

Kipfels turned into "croissants" in 1770 when fifteen-year-old Austrian princess Marie Antoinette arrived in France to marry the future King Louis XVI. Parisian bakers started turning out kipfels in her honor, and the French found themselves in love with a breakfast treat that they soon made their own.

WAR OF JENKINS' EAR

The oddly named conflict that inspired an American land-mark.

No war in history has a more striking title than the War of Jenkins' Ear. Robert Jenkins was a British sea captain whose ship was boarded by the Spanish Coast Guard in the Caribbean. According to Jenkins, the Spanish captain tied him up and cut off his ear with a sword. He was so angry that he brought the severed ear to Parliament, prompting the prime minister to declare war on Spain.

Actually, things were a little more complicated than that. Jenkins didn't exhibit his ear to Parliament until seven years after he said it was cut off. Some people wondered aloud if that shriveled thing in the box really was his severed ear. Critics claimed he had lost his ear in a bar fight, and that the whole thing was a political stunt designed to force a war the prime minister didn't really want.

Whatever the truth, the alleged brutality inflamed public opinion. England was enraged, and war was waged.

The British hero of this war was Admiral Edward Vernon. Today we remember him less for his exploits, perhaps, than for what he inspired.

Admiral Vernon was known as "Old Grog" because he wore a grogram (gross-grain) cloak in stormy weather. After he diluted his sailors' rum ration with water, the disgruntled seamen named the watered-down drink after their commander: grog

One of his officers was a young colonial who owned a farm in Virginia called the Little Hunting Plantation. Lawrence Washington was so impressed with his superior officer that he renamed the farm in Vernon's honor. When Lawrence died a few years later, his younger half brother George inherited the place.

Mount Vernon. Home of President George Washington. And America's only monument to the War of Jenkins' Ear.

Vernon achieved fame for his attack on the Spanish colonial town of Porto Bello, now a part of Panama. He attacked with just six men-of-war and emerged victorious. Londoners are reminded of the battle (or should be) when they go shopping on tony Portobello Road.

A DANDY TALE

A soldiers' song that made history by switching sides.

During the French and Indian War, a British surgeon named Richard Schuckburg put pen to paper to write some new words to an old folk tune. Schuckburg had the reputation for being a delicious wit. Soon his lyrics, which ridiculed colonial militiamen fighting alongside British soldiers, were on everybody's lips.

"Yankee Doodle Dandy."

In the years leading up to the American Revolution this song of insult became a favorite of British soldiers serving in North America. They dreamed up countless new verses mocking the colonials they were growing to detest, as a way of putting those uncouth Americans in their place.

On April 19, 1775, as British troops marched out from Boston to Lexington and Concord, fife and drum played the tune while soldiers sang merrily along. Later in the day as they found themselves in a desperate battle with an army of rebels, the song could be heard again.

But this time it was the colonials who were singing it, throwing the insulting tune back in the face of the British troops as they retreated back to Boston under heavy fire. "Damn them," said one British officer later, "they made us dance it till we were tired." After that it never sounded as sweet to British ears again.

Colonists claimed it as their own, sometimes

Macaroni

referring to it now as the "Lexington March," and taking a new delight in the self-mocking words. The song came to haunt the British, who had to listen to it being played when they surrendered at Saratoga and Yorktown.

And that's how a ditty written to ridicule became America's first national song.

The origin of the word "Yankee" is disputed, but the most likely explanation is that it is from the Dutch form of the name Johnnie, "Jancke" (pronounced yan-kee), which was used by Dutch colonists in New Amsterdam as a dismissive word for English residents of New England.

YANKEE DOODLE CAME TO TOWN
RIDING ON A PONY,
STUCK A FEATHER IN HIS HAT,
AND CALLED HIM MACARONI.

Dozens, if not hundreds, of verses were written for the song in colonial times. These lines, among the earliest, refer to a class of foppish dandies in London who wore outlandish clothes and tried to throw around Italian phrases to show how cultured they were. They were called "Macaronies."

" IT WAS NOT A LITTLE MORTIFYING TO HEAR THEM PLAY THIS TUNE, WHEN THEIR ARMY MARCHED DOWN TO OUR SURRENDER. "

—BRITISH OFFICER TOM ANBURY, FOLLOWING THE BRITISH SURRENDER AT SARATOGA

OLD MAN'S FIGHT

Respect your elders . . . especially when they're armed!

War is usually considered a young man's endeavor. But on April 19, 1775, the first day of the American Revolution, the older generation got their licks in too.

At the battles of Lexington and Concord, colonial militia clashed with the dread Redcoats and sent them fleeing back to Boston. One militiaman who answered the call that day was Samuel Whittemore.

Whittemore was seventy-eight years old and crippled, but that wasn't going to stop him. He headed out to join the fight, and he didn't go lightly armed, either. He carried a rifle, two pistols, and an old cavalry saber.

As the British approached, he took up a position behind a stone wall and got off such accurate fire that the British sent a detachment to rout him out. As they drew close, the old man killed one with a rifle, and shot two more with his pistol. He was reaching for his cavalry saber when they finally fell upon him. One British soldier shot him in the face, while others, whipped into a frenzy, bayoneted him time after time.

Samuel Whittemore suffered fourteen separate wounds. When he was brought to a doctor, the man just shook his head. It was clear that Whittemore had little chance of surviving.

But Samuel Whittemore defied the odds and lived on. He lived long enough to see the British defeated, the Constitution ratified, and George Washington become president. He was ninety-six when he finally died, a remarkable eighteen years after the battle in which that senior soldier fought to make America free.

In another episode, a group of old men ambushed a British ammunition wagon, gunning down two British soldiers and driving off the rest. Several of the soldiers fleeing the ambush came upon an impoverished old woman named Mother Bathrick and begged her to accept their surrender and escort them to safety. This led critics of the war back in England to pose this rhetorical question: "If one old Yankee woman can take six Grenadiers, how many soldiers will it take to conquer America?"

FIGHTING WORDS

The outdated weapon that we can't stop talking about.

The flintlock was invented in France in 1610 and came to American shores shortly thereafter. For more than 200 years, the flintlock played a major role in American history. Flintlock muskets and pistols were the weapons of choice in the American Revolution, the War of 1812, and the Civil War.

And though they have been obsolete for more than a century, they live on in our language.

To fire a flintlock, the shooter first cocked the hammer partway so that he could sprinkle some powder onto the priming pan—but he had to remember to cock the hammer the rest of way before firing. Otherwise the gun would *go off half-cocked.*

When the trigger was pulled, the hammer brought down a piece of flint with great force, creating a shower of sparks. If the powder in the pan ignited but failed to set off the charge inside the barrel, the result was a showy but useless *flash in the pan.*

When that happened, no one knew when or if the gun was going to go off. It was said to be *hanging fire.*

By the way, the "lock" in flintlock referred to the firing mechanism. It was one of three major parts of the gun: only if you had the *lock, stock, and barrel* did you have everything.

Remember the flintlock!

It was a flintlock rifle that fired the "shot heard round the world" on April 19, 1775, that began the American Revolution.

The most famous flintlock was the "Brown Bess," used by British soldiers for more than a century, and eventually immortalized by Rudyard Kipling:

Brown Bess was a partner whom none could despise . . .

With a habit of looking men straight in the eyes.

At Blenheim and Ramillies, fops would confess

They were pierced to the heart by the charms of Brown Bess.

THE GENERAL'S GAMBIT

A bold deception gave George Washington his first victory in the American Revolution.

After spending the winter holed up in Cambridge, General George Washington was determined to drive the British from Boston. One morning when the Redcoats there awoke, they were shocked to find that the hills looking down on Boston were bristling with cannon. Washington was throwing down the gauntlet, his guns poised to blow the enemy to kingdom come.

The British chose not to fight. They evacuated ten thousand men and two hundred warships. Boston was free without a shot being fired.

But what the British didn't know was that Washington's gambit was an enormous bluff. Despite the awesome display of force, he lacked one key ingredient to back it up: gunpowder.

Washington was so short on gunpowder that his army would have been able to throw only a few shots at the British before retreating. So severe, in fact, was the colonial powder shortage that the British could have easily taken Washington's army and crushed the nascent rebellion any time during the previous six months.

If only they had known, American history might have taken a very different turn.

Washington may have lacked gunpowder, but he proved to have something more important: the nerve and audacity that would be needed to see the Revolution through to the finish.

Shortly after taking command of the army in June of 1775, Washington discovered that he had only enough gunpowder for each soldier to fire a handful of bullets. Brigadier General John Sullivan described the moment. "The General was so struck that he did not utter a word for half an hour."

TO MAINTAIN A POST WITHIN MUSKET SHOT OF THE ENEMY FOR SIX MONTHS TOGETHER WITHOUT POWDER . . . IS MORE THAN PROBABLY EVER WAS ATTEMPTED.

—GEORGE WASHINGTON, IN A LETTER
TO CONGRESS, JANUARY 1776

Gunpowder was in short supply because the British had long discouraged its manufacture in the colonies. The problem was eventually eased by importing large quantities from French traders. But even five years later, just before the Battle of Yorktown, Washington's supply of powder was reported to be in a "wretched and palsied state."

With Washington's cannons frowning down on them, Lord Howe and his British army completed their evacuation of Boston by sea in less than two weeks.

FORGOTTEN FIGHT

*Big battle in the
Big Apple.*

The biggest battle of the American Revolution is, oddly enough, also one of the least remembered. It was fought on the streets of New York. The British invasion fleet contained more than four hundred ships and transports carrying thirty-five thousand soldiers and sailors, the biggest British Expeditionary Force until World War I. Facing them were twenty-five thousand inexperienced men under the command of George Washington, who himself had never led a large army into battle.

It was the first and only full-scale conflict of the war. From August until November of 1776, these two armies clashed in a series of engagements that ranged across Brooklyn, up and down the streets of Manhattan, into Harlem and Westchester, and finally across to New Jersey.

It's largely forgotten today, for a simple reason: the colonials suffered a crushing defeat. Washington lost more than three-quarters of his army. Who would want to remember that?

The battle, however, deserves to be remembered. This is where America could have lost the fight for independence in an afternoon . . . but didn't. Instead, it became the place where an army of green soldiers began to learn the trade of war.

The Battle of Trenton, fought by Washington's decimated army a few weeks later, is celebrated as a great American victory. The Continental Army won that fight using lessons learned the hard way in the battle for New York.

The most famous casualty of the battle was a captain from a Connecticut regiment named Nathan Hale, remembered romantically as the spy who "had but one life to give his country." The British viewed him far less romantically: they believed that in addition to being a spy, Hale was one of the colonial arsonists who had torched New York days before, destroying one-quarter of the city.

The British came ashore in Brooklyn, using landing craft that they had constructed on Staten Island. The boats had hinged bows that could be let down and used as ramps, much like the Higgins boats of World War II.

MIRACLE AT SARATOGA

*The debt of gratitude
we owe to a most
unlikely hero.*

On a hillside near Saratoga, New York, a bitter battle was raging between a ragtag American army and crack British troops. One of the Americans' best officers was stewing on the sidelines. He'd been quarreling with the commanding general for days, and just hours before, he had been dismissed for insubordination.

But once the battle began, the headstrong officer couldn't stay away. Damning his orders, he downed a slug of rum, leaped onto a borrowed horse, and raced up to the front lines, saber flashing! Men rallied around him, and he led them into the teeth of British fire. He galloped his horse from one part of the field to another, under constant fire, leading devastating attacks on enemy positions. A bullet shattered his leg and down he went—but not before helping to rout the Redcoats.

The victory at Saratoga, proving as it did that the British were not invincible, convinced France to enter the war on America's side. That turned out to be the key to ultimate triumph. Thanks in large part to the heroic officer who just a few years later would make his name a synonym for treachery and betrayal:

Benedict Arnold.

In joining the battle, Arnold waved his sword so wildly that he inadvertently injured one of his fellow officers.

It was just three years later that Arnold, angry at what he felt was shabby treatment by Congress, offered to hand over the American fort at West Point to the British for £20,000. When the plan was found out, he escaped to a waiting British ship and later became a brigadier general in the British army.

The American commander at Saratoga, Horatio Gates, didn't have to be introduced to defeated British general Johnny Burgoyne at the surrender ceremony. They had both been junior officers in the same British regiment thirty years before.

TRICK OR TREASON

A frontier folk hero accused of being a traitor.

Daniel Boone: charged with treason and facing the gallows. It doesn't quite fit with his heroic image, but that's what happened during the American Revolution.

Captured by Shawnee Indians in 1778, Boone convinced the other members of his hunting party to surrender to the Shawnee without firing a shot. He was then overheard conspiring with the Shawnee and British officers to surrender the town of Boonesboro, Kentucky, which he himself had founded. One of the captives even said Boone took an oath of allegiance to the British.

All of this painted a picture of treachery and betrayal. After returning to Boonesboro, Boone was placed under house arrest, charged with treason, and tried by court-martial.

DANIEL BOONE

Surprisingly, Boone denied none of the facts. But he said it was part of a "stratagem" to deceive the British and save Boonesboro. He got captured by the Indians himself, he said, because he was in his mid-forties and not as fast as he used to be. He surrendered the hunting party rather than see them all get killed. He had spun tales to the British and Indians to buy time, so that he could escape and warn the town.

While other captives were treated badly and forced to run the gauntlet, Boone was adopted by the Shawnee chief and given the name Big Turtle. This alone convinced several of the other captives, who were later ransomed, that Boone had betrayed them. But the incident may just have been one example of Boone's legendary survival skills.

Boone must have been convincing, because he was found innocent on all charges. But hard feelings remained. The famous frontiersman moved away from Boonesboro a year later, leaving the treason charges behind him, and traveling a path that would one day see him elevated into an American legend.

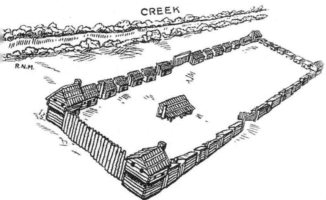

Boone founded Boonesboro in 1775, after leading a party that blazed a trail through the Cumberland Gap and built the Wilderness Road.

BULLDOG OF THE BLACK SEA

The last cruise of
Admiral Pavel.

In 1788, Catherine the Great appointed a combative new commander to a squadron of Russian warships. "One more bulldog for the Black Sea," said the Russian empress, who charged Rear Admiral Pavel Dzhones with the task of liberating that body of water from the Turks.

Admiral Pavel took command of twelve warships at the mouth of the Dnieper River and quickly lived up to Catherine's expectations. His mastery of tactics enabled him to prevail over larger Turkish forces in several engagements, and he demonstrated great personal courage by leading his own ship alongside a Turkish galley to engage in fierce hand-to-hand combat.

The admiral hoped his efforts would bring him great fame. "Loving glory," he wrote to Catherine, "I am perhaps too attached to honors." But it wasn't to be. Back-stabbing colleagues reaped the credit he deserved. He was dismissed from his command and never went to sea again.

But while political intrigue denied Admiral Pavel the chance to become a revered Russian hero, he is remembered for earlier exploits on different oceans. For the man who fought his last battles under the Russian flag was Scottish by birth and American by choice, a fighting captain whose stirring victories in the American Revolution live on today.

His service as a Russian admiral is long forgotten. His immortal words "I have not yet begun to fight" can never be forgotten.

Pavel Dzhones: John Paul Jones.

Jones's finest hour came in 1779. Commanding the Bonhomme Richard, *he fought a fierce three-hour battle with the larger British ship* Serapis *off the coast of England. Called upon to strike his flag and surrender, he famously refused and eventually won the battle even though his own ship was so badly damaged that it later sank.*

America's first naval hero was born John Paul. The Scottish-born captain of a merchant ship in the Caribbean, he killed a sailor during an attempted mutiny in 1773. He fled to the colony of Virginia to avoid trial and added the name Jones to further cover his trail.

D id Jones actually utter the phrase he is credited with, "I have not yet begun to fight"? An officer aboard the *Bonhomme Richard* recalled those were the words Jones used—but his account came forty-six years later. Several accounts written shortly after the battle have Jones saying, "I may sink, but I'll be damned if I strike." And another eyewitness wrote that Jones shouted, "Yankees do not haul down their colors until they are fairly beaten." Whatever his actual words, his spirited refusal to give up was more than clear.

REVOLUTIONARY PENCIL

How a wartime crisis transformed the way we write.

In 1794, just five years after the French Revolution, France was at war with just about everyone else in Europe: England, Spain, Prussia, and Austria. Worse still, the beleaguered French were in short supply of a precious military weapon.

Pencils.

Quill pens were messy and hard to use, especially for an army on the move. If you wanted to jot down a message or sketch enemy fortifications, a pencil was invaluable. But the graphite needed to make pencil lead was found mostly in England and Prussia—now France's enemies. With a dwindling supply of graphite, and no way to get more, France faced a potential paucity of pencils.

The French minister of war decided to draw on the expertise of a highly talented inventor named Nicolas-Jacques Conté.

Conté's idea was to make a little graphite go a long way by grinding it into a fine powder and mixing it with something else. But what? Other inventors had tried glue, gum, shellac, even whale oil—but none worked.

The inventor experimented for eight days and nights without stopping. Finally, he discovered the answer. He combined the graphite with clay, pressed the mixture into molds, and then fired them inside a kiln. The result: dozens of pencils from a very small amount of graphite. Conté's new method was a stunning success. It is still the way pencils are made today.

In January 1795, Conté obtained French patent number 32. And the modern pencil was born.

Conté saved the day for Napoleon during his invasion of Egypt in 1798. When the French army lost much of its munitions and instruments after one battle, Conté put his genius to work improvising all sorts of machines and tools that enabled the army to keep fighting.

Conté discovered that using more clay created a harder pencil, less clay a softer pencil. He designed four grades of pencil—the origin of the schoolchild's no. 2.

AMERICA'S WORST GENERAL

Drunkard,
traitor, thief,
incompetent . . .
and Commander of
the U.S. Army.

We all know America's great generals: Washington, Grant, and Eisenhower, to name but a few. Chances are, however, you've never heard of the man who may well be America's worst general.

His name was James Wilkinson, and his résumé is a litany of corruption and treachery.

- During the American Revolution he plotted to overthrow General Washington. Later he conspired with Aaron Burr to lop off a few states and turn them into an independent country. (He eventually informed on Burr to save his own skin.)

- While serving as a U.S. Army general he also spied on America for Spain. (Spanish archives show that "Agent 13," as they called him, was well paid for his reports. He even took an oath of allegiance to the king of Spain.)

- Appointed "clothier general" of the army, he had to resign the post after an audit suggested he was siphoning off money for himself.

- He was such a military bumbler that during an invasion of Canada in the War of 1812, his force of 4,000 was repulsed by a mere 180 Canadians. (Of course, he was so high on alcohol and laudanum that he may not have noticed.)

In spite all the scandals, he rose through the ranks to become

commander in chief of the American army in 1796. He was a master of intrigue, an expert at covering his tracks, and a consummate flatterer who cultivated friends in high places. Three courts-martial, several congressional investigations, and numerous boards of inquiry failed to lay a finger on him.

General James Wilkinson: a scoundrel, a sneak, a spy—and a survivor.

A GENERAL WHO NEVER WON A BATTLE OR LOST A COURT-MARTIAL.

—HISTORIAN ROBERT LECKIE

I WOULD RATHER BE SHOT THAN SERVE UNDER WILKINSON.

—PRESIDENT JAMES MONROE

THE MOST FINISHED SCOUNDREL THAT EVER LIVED.

—VIRGINIA CONGRESSMAN JOHN RANDOLPH

A TRAITOR TO EVERY CAUSE HE EMBRACED.

—HISTORIAN SAMUEL ELIOT MORRISON

BLIND MAN'S BLUFF

It's the orders you disobey that make you famous.

Horatio Nelson. Admiral Nelson. Lord Nelson. Perhaps the most famous and revered officer ever to tread the deck of a British naval vessel, he is best known for his famous victory at Trafalgar in 1805. It was there, aboard the HMS *Victory*, that he signaled to all his ships that "England expects every man to do his duty." It was there he defeated Napoleon's fleet, saving England from invasion, before dying from wounds suffered in the battle.

But it was at another battle, four years earlier, that he added a colorful phrase to the English language.

At the Battle of Copenhagen, Nelson was second in command to an elderly admiral named Sir Hyde Parker. Nelson led a squadron of ships on a daring attack against the Danish fleet. Soon he was heavily engaged.

From his flagship several miles away, Admiral Parker became convinced that Nelson's squadron was being decimated, that the battle was lost. He hoisted a signal flag ordering Nelson to withdraw. The younger admiral, knowing his ships were inflicting heavy damage on the Danes, paid no attention. When one of his officers pointed it out, Nelson reportedly raised his telescope to his eye and said, "I really do not see the signal." Then he proceeded with the battle.

But the officer knew, as eventually everyone in England knew, that Nelson had put the telescope to his blind eye. Thus Nelson was able to claim ignorance of the order without disobeying it outright. Within the hour he had won a great victory, and given birth to a new expression. So the next time you "turn a blind eye" to something, remember the famous British admiral who did it first.

Danish losses in the Battle of Copenhagen were six thousand killed and wounded, more than ten times the British casualties. The victory earned Nelson a promotion and command of his own fleet.

I HAVE ONLY ONE EYE—I HAVE A RIGHT TO BE BLIND SOMETIMES.

—ADMIRAL NELSON TO HIS FLAG CAPTAIN DURING THE BATTLE

THE FEVER FACTOR

How an island rebellion and a lowly insect helped remake America.

Napoleon Bonaparte had big plans for the vast territory that France held in North America. In 1802 he sent an army under the command of General Charles Leclerc, his brother-in-law, to take control of New Orleans and open the door for a new wave of French colonists to populate what he hoped would be a thriving New France.

Napoleon ordered Leclerc to stop off along the way and reestablish French rule in Haiti, which had been wracked by a bloody slave rebellion. The Haitians were no match for the crack French troops, who won control of the island in a matter of weeks. But then a more deadly enemy emerged.

The mosquito.

Spring rains brought clouds of mosquitoes and an outbreak of yellow fever. The local population was largely immune; not so the French soldiers. Tens of thousands perished. Leclerc himself died in October of 1802. Reinforcements arrived, but many of them also succumbed to the disease. Meantime, the freed slaves of Haiti renewed the fight against their weakened enemy, taking a severe toll with persistent guerrilla attacks.

For France, it was nothing short of a debacle. Between the disease and the fighting, an estimated fifty thousand French soldiers died, and the rest surrendered in 1803. With his army gone and his brother-in-law dead, Napoleon gave up on his dreams for the New World, deciding instead to sell France's land in North America to the United States.

The Louisiana Purchase doubled the size of the young country. But it might never have taken place without the resilient rebels and the unmerciful mosquitoes of Haiti.

The slave rebellion in Haiti was led by Toussaint L'Ouverture, a former slave who had established himself there as "Governor-for-Life." He quickly agreed to an armistice with the French, who showed their gratitude by kidnapping him and sending him off to a French prison, where he died before he could see Haiti achieve full independence in 1803.

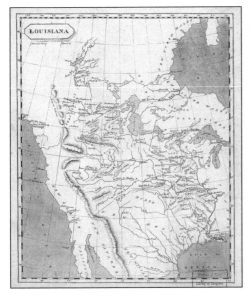

The Louisiana Purchase added 828,000 square miles of land to the United States. The purchase price was $15 million, which comes out to a mere three cents an acre.

It wasn't until nearly one hundred years later that U.S. Army doctor Walter Reed proved that yellow fever is transmitted by mosquitoes.

SHELL SHOCK

*The revolutionary
weapon that
changed warfare
forever.*

At the start of the 1800s, a new weapon appeared on the battlefields of Europe. It was the brainchild of an English officer who had spent thirty years perfecting it. A hollow artillery shell was filled with smaller musket balls, along with a charge of gunpowder ignited by a fuse. The shell could be launched long-distance at the enemy's lines. When it exploded in midair, it spread a deadly carpet of metal shards over a wide area.

The inventor of the shell devoted all his free time to perfecting it, pouring his life savings into the project. The British army finally adopted the shell in 1803, and first used it in the Napoleonic Wars. It proved frighteningly lethal on massed troops, and so terrified French soldiers that they believed the British had poisoned their cannonballs.

Sir George Wood, commander of the British artillery, credited the new shell with playing a critical role in the defeat of Napoleon at the Battle of Waterloo. "On this simple circumstance hinged entirely the turn of the battle," he later wrote in a letter to the shell's inventor.

Artillery became infinitely more terrifying and the name of the officer who invented the shell became known around the world:

Henry Shrapnel.

Shrapnel's shells were the "bombs bursting in air" that Francis Scott Key saw during the bombardment of Fort McHenry in the War of 1812.

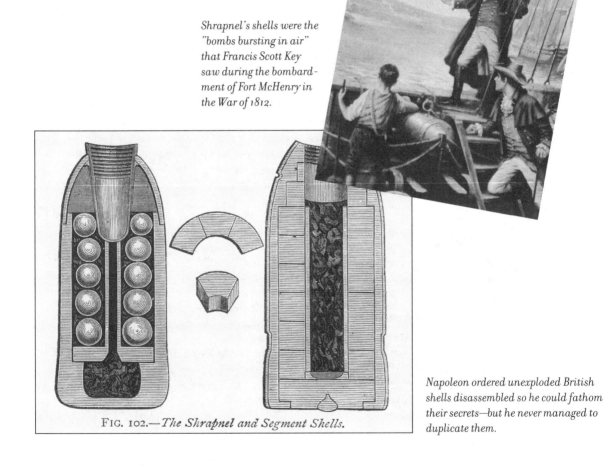

FIG. 102.—*The Shrapnel and Segment Shells.*

Napoleon ordered unexploded British shells disassembled so he could fathom their secrets—but he never managed to duplicate them.

RUM REBELLION

The conflict that was déjà vu all over again.

It was a mutiny. There was no other word for it. It happened in New South Wales, a British penal colony in Australia. A new governor had been sent from London, a man with a quick temper and a keen sense of duty. He soon came into conflict with the colony's officer corps.

The governor considered his officers inept and corrupt, and moved to shut down the thriving rum trafficking ring that they controlled. The officers claimed he was a tyrant and was acting outside of the law. Eventually they decided to depose him. In what later become known as the "Rum Rebellion," three hundred soldiers surrounded his house. They captured him at gunpoint and held him prisoner for more than a year.

Eventually, a dramatic public court-martial in London convicted the mutineers and vindicated the governor.

It was an experience that would have tested any man, but especially one who must have felt that history was repeating itself in a manner most cruel. For the governor of New South Wales was a British naval officer who was discovering that lightning could indeed strike twice.

He was William Bligh, the ship captain famously deprived of his command nearly twenty years before . . . in the mutiny on the *Bounty*.

Bligh was at dinner when he got word that the mutineers were coming to arrest him. He hid out in a small servant's room, hoping to escape. The soldiers who found him claimed he was hiding under a bed, which led to much taunting and accusations of cowardice that seem to have stung Bligh more deeply than the rebellion itself.

The mutiny on the HMS Bounty took place in 1789. Set adrift in a small boat with a handful of loyal seamen and limited supplies, Bligh successfully navigated more than four thousand miles to safety.

THE WAR OF BAD TIMING

It began too quickly and ended too late.

The main cause of the War of 1812 was Britain's interference with American shipping, stemming from a British embargo on trade with France. The United States tried for years to get the British to change the so-called Orders in Council that regulated the hated policies, but to no avail. So finally, on June 18, 1812, the United States declared war.

Bad timing.

It turned out that the British government had revoked the Orders in Council just *two days* before. In other words, the main reason for the war had disappeared. President James Madison later admitted that if he had known of Britain's change of heart, he would have held off declaring war. But it was months before the news reached Washington . . . and by then the die was cast.

Britain and the United States fought for more than two years. The most famous battle of the war was General Andrew Jackson's decisive defeat of the British at the Battle of New Orleans, on January 8, 1815. It made Jackson a national hero, and eventually led to his becoming president.

More bad timing.

The Treaty of Ghent, officially ending the war, was signed on December 24, 1814. The battle, in other words, was fought two weeks after the war was over.

The Battle of New Orleans was the most lopsided of the war. The British attack on American lines along the Mississippi proved a bloody disaster. The British suffered more than two thousand casualties; the American forces, only seventy.

It took two years to fight the war, four and a half months to negotiate the Treaty of Ghent, and five weeks to get the documents from Europe to Washington. After all that time, it took the Senate and the president just one day to unanimously ratify the treaty bringing the war to an end.

AN ARMY OF TWO

How a pair of teenage girls outwitted a British man-of-war.

In June of 1814, the British frigate HMS *Bulwark*, bearing seventy-four guns, raided the Massachusetts town of Scituate, setting fire to six ships in the harbor. The town promptly formed a militia company to protect itself. The men held their drills by the lighthouse, but as the summer went by without any more incidents, they began to let their guard down.

In September, the *Bulwark* came back for another bite.

Rebecca Bates, the eighteen-year-old daughter of the lighthouse keeper, spotted the British ship sitting offshore. A longboat full of soldiers was setting off toward the harbor, where two merchant ships presented a juicy target.

Her father wasn't around. There was no time to get to town to warn of the attack. Then Rebecca noticed something the militiamen had left at the lighthouse, something that gave her an idea: a fife and drum.

The soldiers had taught them a few songs over the summer. Now Rebecca thought they could use one of them to fool the British. "Keep out of sight," she warned her sister. "If they see us, they'll laugh us to scorn." The two girls hid out behind a dune and played "Yankee Doodle" for all they were worth.

The British heard the all too familiar tune wafting over the water. It could mean only one thing: American soldiers were gathering to repel their attack. A signal pennant was hoisted and the raiding party aborted their mission.

Scituate was saved from attack by Rebecca and Abigail Bates, forever known to their town as An American Army of Two.

The handwritten affidavit reads:

Rebecca Bates born 1793 aged 81 years one of the American army of two in the year of 1812 who with her sister aged 15 years, saved two large vessels loaden with flour and their crew from imprisonment with fife and drum from being taken by the British of Scituate Harbour

Rebecca the fifer

Rebecca Bates lived to a great old age and told many people of the day she saved Scituate. She and her sister even signed affidavits swearing to the accuracy of their story.

> ## "YOU TAKE THE DRUM AND I'LL TAKE THE FIFE."

—REBECCA BATES TO HER SISTER ABIGAIL, AS THEY PREPARED TO DRIVE OFF THE BRITISH

"THE STAR-SPANGLED BANNER"

Next time you hear our national anthem, tip your hat to the drunken Redcoats who made it possible.

Washington, D.C., was aflame, thanks to British soldiers who had put it to the torch. With smoke still rising from the ruins, the Brits set out on a march through Maryland. After most of the soldiers had filed peacefully through the town of Upper Marlboro, two drunken stragglers came along shouting and carrying on. One of the town fathers, Dr. William Beanes, was so incensed with this behavior that he personally carted the drunken Redcoats to jail.

But one of the men escaped, and brought back more Redcoats. They released the jailed soldier, seized the good doctor, and carried him off to a British frigate in Chesapeake Bay. So a lawyer friend sailed out to negotiate the doctor's release. Just as he got there, the British began shelling nearby Fort McHenry, and detained both men until the shelling was over.

And that's how a lawyer by the name of Francis Scott Key happened to observe the flag over the fort still standing amidst the "rockets' red glare." His poem, "The Star-Spangled Banner," became an instant hit.

The music? Key purloined it from a tune called "To Anacreon in Heaven," which, appropriately enough, was a popular English drinking song.

Key wrote the poem in a Baltimore hotel room the day after the battle. It was published for the first time less than a week later.

FRANCIS SCOTT KEY.

Mary W. Howe

OUR COUNTRY'S FLAG!
A New National Song.
Words from the
SAVANNAH GEORGIAN
SIGNED ORLANDO.
Music Composed by
Geo. F. Cole.
Published by John Cole & Son, Baltimore.

It took more than forty bills and resolutions in Congress before "The Star-Spangled Banner" was finally adopted as the national anthem in 1931.

BAD DAY AT WATERLOO

Imagine you wake up feeling ill . . . and it costs you an empire.

Napoleon was ready for battle. He faced a host of enemies: a mighty army composed of British, Belgian, Dutch, and German units that had gathered together for the express purpose of destroying him. But Napoleon was the world's greatest general. It would take more than cannon and cavalry to stop him.

It would take an act of nature.

The mighty emperor was sick. Hemorrhoids and a bladder infection struck him with force and fury and did what no earthly army could—render him immobile. In great pain the night before the battle, he took a dose of opium that caused him to sleep late and lose crucial hours that could have made the difference.

The morning of the battle he was in such pain that he could barely mount his horse. Personal reconnaissance of the battlefield was out of the question. Some accounts say he took more opium, which may have clouded his judgment.

The emperor was not at his best, and his day went from bad to worse as he suffered an empire-ending defeat.

If only he could have called in sick.

Who won the Battle of Waterloo? It depends on whom you ask. The English credit the Duke of Wellington, who commanded the combined British, Dutch, and Belgian forces that battled Napoleon most of the day. Bah, say German historians; they argue instead for Marshal Blücher, who arrived on the battle-field in the late afternoon with a Prussian army that delivered the decisive counterpunch. Either way, Napoleon lost.

SPEARHEADING A REVOLUTION

A simple idea with remarkable consequences.

When you throw a spear—and miss—you not only disarm yourself, you give a weapon to your enemy. This radical thought entered the mind of a Zulu warrior sometime shortly after 1800, and his response changed the face of a continent.

The warrior, named Shaka, concluded that the age-old tactic of lofting lightweight spears at enemy formations was next to useless. He devised a new kind of stabbing spear, shorter and heavier, with a bigger blade, which he used to draw close to his enemy and kill them in hand-to-hand combat.

It became known as the *iklwa*—for the sucking sound it made when it was plunged into and pulled out of a human body.

Shaka Zulu used this new method of fighting to become Africa's most famous and feared conqueror, as well as one of the great commanding generals of all time. Starting with just a few men under his command, he ended up ruling an empire and commanding an army of more than fifty thousand. He revolutionized warfare on the African continent, introducing bold new tactics and the concept of total war.

The result was the death of more than two million Africans, depopulating a wide swath of southern Africa, just as white settlers were beginning to colonize.

As a boy, Shaka was exiled from his village along with his mother, and he remained unusually close to her. When she died, he ordered thousands of Zulus killed so that their families might mourn along with him. In his deranged grief he ordered that no crops be planted and all pregnant women slain; even milk cows were killed so that their calves might know what it was like to lose a mother.

Shaka was chief of the Zulus from 1816 until 1828, when he was assassinated by his half brother.

" NGADLA! ["I HAVE EATEN!"] "

—CRY OF THE ZULU WARRIOR
AFTER STABBING THE *IKLWA*
INTO AN ENEMY

Zulu warriors wielding their iklwa spears while performing a war dance. Shaka also taught his warriors how to hook the left edge of their shield behind an opponent's shield, then spin him around with a backhand sweep, making him vulnerable to a stabbing thrust.

BUDDING STATESMAN

How a U.S. Secretary of War planted the seed for a Christmas tradition.

Joel Poinsett was an ambassador, a congressman, and eventually Secretary of War from 1837 to 1841. He holds the distinction of being the only U.S. statesman whose name was made into a word in two different languages—meaning two different things.

During Poinsett's years as ambassador to Mexico, he got a little too embroiled in the political intrigues swirling about Mexico City—some even said he was plotting with revolutionaries who wanted to bring down the government. Mexican authorities grew angry at his heavy-handed interference in Mexican affairs, and they coined a new word to describe his officious and intrusive manner: *poinsettismo.*

He was eventually asked to leave Mexico . . . but not before he did something that we commemorate every Christmas to this day.

Poinsett was an avid botanist, and he became enchanted with a flower he found that grew only in southern Mexico. The Aztecs called it *cuetlaxochitl.* He began growing the flowers in his greenhouse, and started shipping samples back to the United States. Eventually the winter-blooming plant became a holiday hit, and the season of peace became a little brighter thanks to the flower that bears the name of a Secretary of War.

Poinsettia.

A California rancher named Paul Ecke pioneered the idea of marketing the poinsettia as a holiday flower in the 1920s. His untiring efforts to promote the poinsettia over the next forty years made it the ubiquitous Christmas flower it is today.

J. R. Poinsett

As Secretary of War, Poinsett helped reorganize the U.S. Army and expanded West Point. He also spearheaded the founding of the Smithsonian. But still, it is with a flower that he made the greatest impact.

DAVY'S DEATH

The final moments of an American hero.

For many, the enduring image of the Battle of the Alamo is Davy Crockett fighting like a wildcat to the bitter end. According to one dramatic account shortly after his death, his body was found encircled by "seventeen dead Mexicans, eleven of whom had come to their deaths by his dagger and the others by his rifle and four pistols."

So goes the legend. What about the truth?

While the 189 Texans who fought at the Alamo were all killed, numerous Mexican soldiers wrote accounts of the battle. They paint a far different picture of Crockett's last moments.

Mexican general Santa Anna ordered his troops to "give no quarter" when they stormed the Alamo, and the hand-to-hand fighting that followed was bloody and desperate. It lasted until dawn. That's when Crockett and six other men were found, quite alive, in a back room, to which they had retreated. Crockett, by one account, then tried to talk his way out, telling his captors he had planned to become a loyal Mexican citizen, and had done no fighting at the Alamo.

When the men were brought to Santa Anna, the general was so enraged that his "take no prisoners" directive had been disobeyed, he ordered his soldiers to execute the captives on the spot. "With swords in hand," wrote one Mexican officer, they "fell upon these unfortunate, defenseless men just as a tiger leaps upon his prey."

The truth was known within weeks of the battle, and published in many newspapers. But the myth proved far more appealing, and so endures to this day.

That Crockett fought bravely is not in question. A letter smuggled out of the Alamo recounted that during an initial bombardment, "The Hon. David Crockett was seen at all points, animating men to do their duty." But there is no evidence to support the legend of his fighting to his very last moments.

While Crockett carefully cultivated his image as a backwoodsman, he was well on his way to becoming a career politician. He spent four years in the Tennessee Legislature and six in the U.S. Congress before he was voted out of office. He came to Texas in hopes of replenishing his finances and jump-starting his political career.

Mexican general Manuel Fernande Castrillón recognized the famous frontiersman and pleaded with Santa Anna to spare the captives. An indignant Santa Anna refused, saying, "Have I not told you before how to dispose of them? Why do you bring them to me?" Then he ordered the execution.

TEA PARTY

How did Britain's thirst for tea lead to a drug war in China?

At the beginning of the 1700s, virtually no one in Britain drank tea. By the end of the 1700s, everyone did. The British were gulping down tea as fast as the East India Company could import it from China. It was a national love affair.

But there was a problem. The Chinese weren't particularly interested in importing European trade goods, so by the early 1800s it required the modern equivalent of a billion dollars a year in hard currency to pay for the tea. Silver and gold were flowing out of England to China, creating a terrible problem in foreign debt.

The solution? The East India Company, in collusion with the British government, became the world's biggest drug dealer. The company started producing massive amounts of opium in India, and worked out a complex scheme to smuggle it into China to trade for the tea. Opium shipments increased by a factor of 250. By 1839, widespread opium addiction was a serious problem in China.

The emperor of China tried to put a stop to the drug trade that was ruining his country. His agents destroyed British stocks of opium in the trading port of Canton and kicked the British out. But would Britain stand for that?

Not for all the tea in China.

Britain responded by going to war to protect its opium trade. The Opium War was an easy victory for the British, who forced China to let the trade continue for another seventy years.

The result: millions of Chinese addicted to opium in order to subsidize Britain's love for tea.

One of the consequences of the Opium War was that the British took control of Hong Kong, which remained in their hands until 1999.

The freshest tea commanded the highest price, so the tea trade launched a fleet of "clipper" ships, fast cargo vessels that would race across the ocean, to see who could get the first tea of the season back to London the fastest. One of the most famous was the Cutty Sark, which could carry more than a million pounds of tea, and sail from China to England in under a hundred days.

SPENCER'S LEGACY

A hanging at sea that led to the creation of the Naval Academy.

Philip Spencer was a fresh-faced twenty-year-old the day he was hanged. Spencer was a screw-up. He had pretty much flunked out of two colleges before his father pulled strings to get him an appointment as a midshipman (an officer in training) in the U.S. Navy. True to form, Spencer promptly got himself kicked off a ship for drinking.

Given a second chance on the brig *Somers*, he allegedly hatched a plot with some crewmates to take over the ship. Accused of mutiny by the captain, Spencer said he was just joking. "It was only a fancy," he said.

Spencer and two confederates were chained to the quarterdeck. The *Somers* was hundreds of miles from port, the crew was angry and resentful, and it seemed to the officers that at any moment the sailors might rise up to murder them and free the three prisoners.

So Captain Alexander Slidell McKenzie ordered that Spencer and his two co-conspirators be hanged from the yardarm.

But Philip Spencer was not just any young man. His father was the Secretary of War, and his hanging shocked the nation. Some accused the captain of overreacting. Others wanted to know how an unqualified teenager could get an appointment as a midshipman, then be put aboard ship with no training.

The public called for reform. Just over two years later, in response to the *Somers* affair, a naval school was founded to turn midshipmen into well-trained officers. Philip Spencer could never have imagined that his death might pave the way for the creation of the U.S. Naval Academy.

> As a student at Union College, Philip Spencer and a group of friends founded the Chi Psi fraternity, which has chapters at thirty-two American colleges and universities today. "He always took a great delight in the initiations, grips, signs, and passwords," wrote one of his fellow students years later, "and studied how to make them more mysterious and impressive."

Secretary of War John Spencer was in the forefront of those demanding a court-martial for Captain McKenzie, but a navy court eventually exonerated him. McKenzie's naval career was effectively over, however, and he was never trusted with command of another warship.

Philip Spencer and his co-conspirators were the last men ever to be hanged aboard a U.S. naval vessel. Spencer was also the inspiration for the title character in Herman Melville's novel Billy Budd.

TERROR FROM THE SKIES

*The modest begin-
nings of modern
airpower.*

Squadrons of bombers overhead wreaking havoc on targets below—a common feature of modern warfare. But in March of 1849, it was just a crazy idea in the mind of an Austrian artillery offi cer.

The Austrian army was besieging Venice as part of the War of Italian Indepen-dence. The marshy lagoons surrounding the island city made it difficult for the Austrians to bring up their big guns in order to bombard the Venetians into submission. That's when Lieutenant Uchatius put forward an idea brand-new in the annals of warfare.

Why not drop bombs from the sky?

The Austrians organized two "Aerial Torpedo Squadrons." Each contained one hundred unmanned hot-air balloons and one hundred bombs, which were equipped with fuses to release the bombs at a predetermined time. Small pilot balloons were launched to determine wind speed and direction, enabling the Austrians to calculate a departure point and fuse time that they hoped would drop the bombs right over Venice.

After months of preparation, the attack began in July. Some of the balloons were launched from a frigate anchored off Venice—the very first projection of airpower from a ship.

It was an idea ahead of its time. The bombs did little damage to Venice, and when a fickle wind blew some of the balloons back over Austrian lines, the operation was halted for good. The day of the bomber was still ahead, but a thoroughly modern tool of death and destruction had been born.

Eventually, after the balloon bombing failed, the Austrians managed to bring up their guns and bombarded Venice the old-fashioned way. The city surrendered shortly afterward.

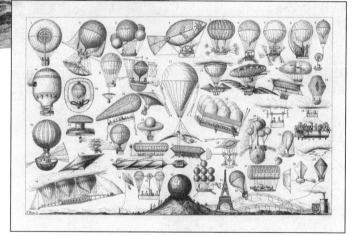

The Russians actually tried to become the first aerial bombers in 1812. Emperor Alexander I ordered the construction of a huge fish-shaped balloon capable of carrying men and explosives. The idea was to hover over Napoleon's headquarters and drop a bomb on it. The fins designed to steer the balloon, however, could not be made to work, and the attempt was abandoned.

The initial idea for the aerial bombardment of Venice was to control the balloon bombs with long copper wires, using an electric battery to launch the bomb from the ground once the balloon was over the target. But this proved to be impractical.

THE ART OF WAR

Painting a picture of military failure.

The cadet had suffered his share of problems at West Point. Truthfully, the main reason he was there was because his widowed mother wanted him to become a career military officer like his late father.

His first year, he got enough demerits to be kicked out. But the superintendent of the academy, a soon-to-be-famous colonel named Robert E. Lee, was kind enough to forgive some of his demerits and allow him to continue.

In his second year he fell gravely ill, and Colonel Lee had to write his mother to come get him. After he recovered, though, he passed all his exams, even coming in number one in his drawing class. Things were finally looking up.

And then, at the end of his third year, came the fateful exam. It was an oral exam, in chemistry, and it may go down as the shortest oral exam in West Point history. The instructor asked the young man to discuss silicon.

"Silicon is a gas," began the cadet.

"That will do," the instructor interrupted him. With four words the cadet had managed to fail chemistry and flunk out of West Point. "Had silicon been a gas," he said later, "I would have been a Major-General."

But what the military world lost, the art world gained. The cadet put his skill at drawing and painting to good use, becoming one of America's most renowned artists: James McNeill Whistler.

And his mother, Anna, who wished for him a career in the military? She is remembered as his most famous subject:

Whistler's mother.

Apparently, a girl Whistler was painting had an accident and was no longer available to pose. Whistler asked his mother to fill in. After posing standing for several days, she became so exhausted that Whistler let her sit down, and completed the painting with her sitting. He eventually had to pawn the painting for cash. It is now displayed at the Musée d'Orsay in Paris.

O ther famous West Point flunk-outs include author and poet Edgar Allan Poe and 1960s drug guru Timothy Leary.

DRESSED TO KILL...
OR BE KILLED

*The military
fiasco that was
a fashion boon.*

The Charge of the Light Brigade took place during the Battle of Balaklava in the Crimean War. Both battle and war have been largely forgotten, but the charge lives on, thanks to Alfred Lord Tennyson's famous poem.

*Into the valley of Death
Rode the six hundred.*

There was some confusion about the orders, and 673 British cavalrymen were sent on a doomed charge up a long valley with Russian artillery firing on them from all sides.

*Theirs not to reason why;
Theirs but to do and die.*

In less than twenty minutes, the Light Brigade was decimated. More than two hundred men were killed. Militarily, it was a terrible blunder. But it quickly captured the imagination of the British public, who regarded it not as a disaster, but as something glorious and noble. The commander of the Light Brigade, James Thomas Brudenell, was lionized as a national hero.

He also inspired a piece of clothing we still use today.

Brudenell bought his men button-down collarless sweaters they could wear under their uniform to keep warm. After the battle, the style became all the rage, and it was named after him.

Never heard of the Brudenell sweater, you say? That's because it was named after his title. Thomas Brudenell was an earl. In fact, he was the seventh Earl of . . . Cardigan.

Everyone remembers the Charge of the Light Brigade, but no one recalls the Charge of the Heavy Brigade from the same battle. Tennyson wrote a poem about that too, but it's virtually unknown. Maybe that's because the Heavy Brigade scored an easy success instead of a romantic failure.

Cardigan's superior officer, who gave the order for the charge, was also a fashion inspiration. After he lost an arm at the Battle of Waterloo, Lord Raglan began wearing a capelike coat with sleeves extending to the neck. The raglan sleeve is still a popular style today.

It was eight years before the Crimean War that a British officer named Harry Lumsden made fashion history of his own. Tasked with organizing an elite unit of Pashtun tribesmen in India, Lumsden decided to forgo the army's traditional scarlet uniforms and outfitted his men in something less obtrusive: lightweight clothing the color of mud. The uniforms were named after the Hindu word for dust: *khak*. And that's how khakis were born.

1855

OVER THE HUMP?

How the West was almost won.

Imagine this Old West scene: the cavalry rides to the rescue, on the backs of their trusty . . . camels? It might have come to pass if an unusual army experiment had turned out differently.

In 1855, U.S. Secretary of War Jefferson Davis convinced Congress to give the army thirty thousand dollars to import camels for military use. Davis believed camels might prove more useful than horses and mules in the harsh, desert-like conditions that prevailed across much of the western United States.

A total of seventy-eight camels were brought from the Middle East to Texas. They quickly proved their worth. The camels could carry more than a thousand pounds on their backs, go days or weeks without water, move faster than horses, and eat desert vegetation that other animals wouldn't touch. Along with their humps, though, camels also came with downsides. Their powerful aroma drove horses and mules crazy, while their screeching, spitting, and biting made army drivers absolutely hate them.

Nonetheless, in 1858 a new Secretary of War, John Floyd, was so enthusiastic about the use of camels that he asked Congress to embrace the idea on a grand scale, and import a thousand camels for military use. Floyd believed the superiority of the camel would convince Indians they could never escape the cavalry, and encourage them to give up raiding.

But Congress had other things on its mind. The call for camels fell by the wayside as rising tensions between North and South consumed the country. After the Civil War broke out, the army's dabbling in dromedaries was all but forgotten; the camel cavalry never made it over that initial hump.

The hump of a camel is fatty tissue that absorbs water and stores it. Normally a camel will drink every three days, twenty to thirty gallons at a time, but camels have been known to go an extraordinary ten months without water.

After the war, the remaining army camels were sold off. Eventually many of them were turned loose in Arizona, Texas, and Nevada, where they reverted to a wild state. The last sighting of wild camels was in 1905, in Arizona.

Secretary of War Jefferson Davis, who would one day become president of the Confederate States of America, was so enthralled by the possible military uses of camels that he and his wife translated a book on the subject from French into English.

BITE THE BULLET

The revolutionary weapon that triggered a revolution.

For 150 years, the British East India Company ruled India through an army of native soldiers (known as Sepoys) commanded by British officers. In the 1850s, the officers began distributing a state-of-the-art firearm to their men: the Enfield rifle.

It was a decision that would soon backfire.

Instead of old-fashioned musket balls, the Enfield fired the new conical Minie bullet, giving the rifle increased range and accuracy. Bullet and powder were contained in a paper cartridge, which was heavily greased to keep the powder dry. Loading the rifle required biting off the end of the greased cartridge to expose the gunpowder.

Big problem.

Word spread among the troops that the grease contained fat from pigs and cows, meaning that biting the cartridge was a sacrilege for both Hindus and Moslems. In May of 1857, eighty-five Sepoys in the town of Meerut refused to use the new rifles. They were stripped of their uniforms and sentenced to ten years at hard labor. Outraged by what they saw as religious persecution, fellow soldiers rose up and killed their British officers, then freed their comrades.

India was already seething with discontent, and this mutiny launched a full-scale rebellion. Violence quickly spread as Indian princes and oppressed peasants joined the revolution. Thousands died, with atrocities on both sides.

In the end, the British government brutally suppressed the rebellion, and

took direct control of the country. But as costly and unsuccessful as it was, the mutiny triggered by a new kind of rifle planted the seeds of a nationalist movement that would eventually make India independent one hundred years later.

Sepoys massacred British soldiers and their families at Cawnpore, hacking them to death even after they had surrendered. When the British retook the town, they forced their prisoners to lick the blood off the floor before taking them out and hanging them.

The British indulged in their own cruelties, inventing a punishment known as the "Devil's Wind." They would lash a man to a cannon and fire a cannonball through his body, blowing him to bits, and thus demolishing his hope for an afterlife.

Like so many culture clashes, this one was born of ignorance and mistrust. The British believed they were showing faith in the men by giving them their newest rifle, while many Sepoys believed the greased cartridges were part of a plot to force them to become Christians by first making them outcasts from their own religions.

RED CROSS

The bloody battle that gave birth to a mission of mercy.

L ittle remembered today, the Battle of Solferino was one of the most terrible in history. On June 24, 1859, French and Italian forces under Napoleon III attacked an Austrian army. Three hundred thousand men engaged in furious fighting for more than fifteen hours.

A Swiss businessman named Henry Dunant who was trying to arrange a meeting with Napoleon III found himself a witness to the battle. He was shocked by the horrifying carnage. "Every mound, every rocky crag is the scene of a fight to the death," he wrote later. "It is sheer butchery."

What came next was even worse. A staggering forty thousand were left wounded on the field of battle, and medical care for them was totally inadequate. Dunant threw himself into the effort to help the wounded, despairing when many died for lack of care. He recalled one wounded soldier who spoke bitterly of his fate: "If I had been looked after sooner I might have lived, and now by evening I shall be dead." And he was.

Terribly moved by what he had seen, Dunant wrote a book about his experiences, and called for the formation of an international organization to provide aid. His work led to the First Geneva Convention and the formation of an international relief agency.

To protect doctors and nurses on the battlefield, the nations who formed the agency also agreed on a symbol that would proclaim its

More than forty years later, Dunant was awarded the first Nobel Peace Prize for his efforts.

neutrality. In a fitting tribute to this compassionate Swiss businessman, they reversed the colors of the Swiss flag to create:

The Red Cross.

> ❝ IS IT NOT A MATTER OF URGENCY, SINCE UNHAPPILY WE CANNOT AVOID WAR, TO PREVENT, OR AT LEAST TO ALLEVIATE, THE HORRORS OF WAR. ❞
>
> —HENRY DUNANT

At the time of the Battle of Solferino, the French army had more veterinarians than it did medical doctors.

THE PIG WAR

The United States and Great Britain on the brink of war . . . over a dead pig?

In 1859, the last bit of territory in dispute by the U.S. and Great Britain was the San Juan Island chain, in the waters between Canada and the Oregon Territory. Both countries claimed the islands, and both had settlers there who eyed each other with suspicion and hostility.

That was the status quo the day Lyman Cutlar, an American living on San Juan Island, shot a pig that was rooting around in his potato patch.

A British pig.

British authorities threatened to arrest Cutlar if he didn't make restitution. After Americans on the island turned to the U.S. Army for help, a hotheaded general named William Harney responded by sending a company of men from the Ninth Infantry. The governor of British Columbia, in turn, ordered a warship to the scene. Both sides escalated. Soon four hundred American soldiers were dug in on the island, while a fleet of British ships carrying thousands of armed men waited just offshore.

The possibility of war seemed very real.

At this point, cooler heads prevailed. British naval officers refused orders to land Royal Marines on the island, thus avoiding a confrontation. The U.S. government, horrified that the actions of one irate farmer could precipitate a war, sent General Winfield Scott, Commander of the U.S. Army, to calm things down. Both parties eventually agreed to a joint occupation of the islands, bringing an end to a military confrontation in which the only casualty was a pig.

The pig shot by Lyman
Cutlar was actually a Berkshire boar.

"We'll make a Bunker Hill of
it," said the army captain
who commanded the U.S.
troops sent to occupy San
Juan Island. But George
Pickett's moment of glory
would come four years later,
as a Confederate general,
when he lent his name to the
most famous—and futile—
charge in American history,
at the Battle of Gettysburg.

> ## RESIST ALL ATTEMPTS AT INTERFER-
> ## ENCE BY THE BRITISH AUTHORITIES.

—INSTRUCTIONS TO THE U.S. TROOPS OCCUPYING SAN JUAN ISLAND

Ten years after the events of the "Pig War," the U.S. and Britain re-
ferred their dispute over the islands to a neutral third party: Kaiser
Wilhelm I of Germany. He eventually ruled in favor of the United
States, and today the islands are part of Washington State.

NATIVE GUARDS

The extraordinary military unit that served on both sides in the Civil War.

The Louisiana Native Guard was a militia regiment formed by eager volunteers in the early days of the Civil War to fight for the South. What made it unique among Confederate military units was the origin of its men.

They were all free blacks living in New Orleans.

Why were they willing to fight for the South? Some saw it as a way to gain equality. Others owned property they were afraid of losing if they refused to fight. Many were mulattoes who identified more with Southern whites than with slaves.

The South didn't permit the Native Guards to go into battle, and used it more for propaganda than anything else. This treatment quickly dampened the unit's enthusiasm for the Confederate cause.

But the men of the Native Guards still desperately wanted to prove themselves. After New Orleans was occupied by the Union, many of the officers and men volunteered to fight for the Union. They were joined by runaway slaves also anxious to take up arms.

And so the Native Guards, reconstituted as three *Union* regiments, became the only unit to serve both the South *and* the North during the Civil War.

They were the first black units in the Union Army, and they fought bravely at the Battle of Port Hudson. In spite

of their performance, they were not well treated by the army. Black officers were replaced with whites, and the men were used primarily for guard duty and manual labor.

Despite their willingness to work and fight, the Native Guards were orphaned by two armies. As one of their officers observed: "Nobody really desires our success."

One of the officers of the Native Guards, P.B.S. Pinchback, served briefly as governor of Louisiana during Reconstruction, making him the state's first and only black governor. Pinchback was one-quarter African-American: the son of a Louisiana planter and his mulatto mistress.

> **R**obert E. Lee suggested recruiting slaves as soldiers in the late days of the Civil War, but the South's view of black troops was summed up by Confederate general Cobb Howell: "If slaves make good soldiers, our whole theory of slavery is wrong."

THEY FOUGHT SPLENDIDLY! SPLENDIDLY! EVERYBODY IS DELIGHTED THAT THEY DID SO WELL.

—GENERAL NATHANIEL P. BANKS ON THE NATIVE GUARDS AT PORT HUDSON

The three Native Guards regiments serving in the Union Army were also known as the "Corps D'Afrique."

TWENTY-FOUR NOTES

The Civil War general who whistled his way into history.

Dan Butterfield was a New York businessman turned Union general. People seemed to love him or hate him. He was awarded the Medal of Honor for rallying his brigade under withering fire, but he had a bad temper that irritated fellow officers. One wrote that he was a man of "blemished character."

Perhaps so. But he also had poetry in his soul.

One night in July of 1862 he called the brigade bugler to his tent. Butterfield wasn't happy with the regulation bugle call played at the end of the day to signal "lights out." It wasn't sufficiently musical, he said.

The general had something different in mind. Since by his own admission he couldn't write a note of music, he whistled it for bugler Oliver Norton. When Norton played it back, the result wasn't quite what Butterfield wanted, and they went back and forth for a while, the general whistling, the bugler blowing, until they had something Butterfield was satisfied with.

Norton used the new call that night. Buglers from other brigades camped nearby were so struck by it that they began using it as well. Soon the call spread throughout the army, and to the Confederate army as well.

And so a collaboration between a general and a bugler on a warm July evening led to twenty-four notes that have gone down in history: a haunting melody known to all that announces the end of day for soldiers and graces the air at military funerals.

Taps.

Slow.

Put out the lights, Go to sleep, Go to sleep, Go to slee

Soldiers began making up words to the song as soon as bugler started playing it. These are some of the earliest.

Butterfield seems to have gotten the idea for the new bugle call from parts of an older call no longer in use, revising it to capture the mood he sought.

Bugler Oliver W. Norton recalled that Butterfield wanted a call that in its music should carry some suggestion of putting out the lights and lying down to rest in the silence of the camp.

THREE CIGARS

The South might have won the Civil War . . . but for three cigars.

September 13, 1862, was a Saturday, but for the soldiers of the Twenty-seventh Indiana Regiment it was just another day of marching. Like the rest of the Union Army under General George McClellan, they were moving down the dirt roads of Maryland, trying to come to grips with Robert E. Lee's Confederate Army, which had invaded the North.

It was a critical time in the war. A decisive victory by Lee could pave the way for a settlement that would lead to recognition of the South as a separate nation. McClellan, slow and overcautious, seemed ill-suited to stop him.

The Twenty-seventh stopped to rest in a field that had been occupied by Confederates just days before. Three soldiers sprawled out on the ground noticed something lying nearby: three cigars wrapped in a piece of paper. Delighted, the soldiers decided to split the cigars. They were about to throw out the wrapper when one of them, Corporal Barton W. Mitchell, thought to take a look at it.

At that moment, the unwitting corporal may have been the most important person on the planet, with thousands of lives and the fate of nations riding on his curiosity.

What Mitchell found in his hands was a copy of the marching orders for Lee's army, apparently lost by a Confederate officer. He promptly passed his discovery up the chain of command. Galvanized by this captured information, McClellan promptly went on the attack.

The result: the Confederates were turned back at the Battle of Antietam, the bloodiest single day in American history. More than five thousand men died in the fighting that day.

All because of three cigars.

This is the paper found by the soldiers, Special Orders 191. They were written out by Lee's assistant adjutant general, R. H. Chilton. By sheer coincidence, one of the Union officers who examined the orders happened to know Chilton before the war and so was able to verify that it was his handwriting, thus convincing General McClellan the document was genuine.

> ## HERE IS A PAPER WITH WHICH IF I CANNOT WHIP BOBBY LEE I WILL BE WILLING TO GO HOME.

—GENERAL GEORGE MCCLELLAN

Another one of the soldiers who found the cigars, Sergeant John Bloss, survived the battle by more than forty years and ended up becoming a much beloved president of Oregon State University. (He's in the front row, second from the right.)

UNLEADED ZEPPELIN

How did the Civil War change the course of aviation history?

Count Ferdinand von Zeppelin was a young Prussian military officer when he was sent to the United States in 1863 as a military observer attached to the Union Army. The enthusiastic young lieutenant rode along on several missions with Union cavalry, and was almost captured by the Confederates a week before the Battle of Gettysburg.

Having come so far, von Zeppelin set out to explore the breadth of the United States. And so it was that he ended up in Minneapolis, where he ran into something that changed his life:

A ride in a balloon.

The balloon was being operated by John Steiner, who had spent a year as an aeronaut for the Union Army. On August 19 he let von Zeppelin go up on a tethered ascent. The young nobleman rose six hundred feet into the air. He was hooked.

Steiner regaled von Zeppelin with tales of doing military reconnaissance over Confederate lines, noting that the biggest problem was the inability to steer the balloon. The answer, Steiner thought, would be to create a cigar-shaped balloon with a rudder that could be easily guided through the air.

Von Zeppelin was soon on his way back to Germany, but he never forgot that balloon ride, or Steiner's idea. Twenty-five years later, after he retired from the army, he set out to build a rigid, steerable ballon. The first Zeppelin made its maiden flight on July 2, 1900, launching a new age of lighter-than-air travel that owed its birth to the War Between the States.

Aeronauts from the Balloon Corps performed valuable reconnaissance for the Union Army. The best known among them was Thaddeus Lowe, whose efforts are credited with helping the Union win the Battle of Fair Oaks.

Zeppelins carried passengers back and forth across the Atlantic in the 1930s, until the Hindenburg exploded over Lakehurst, New Jersey, in 1937, killing thirty-seven people. With that, the age of the airship was over.

The ascent of the LZ-1, the first Zeppelin, in 1900. More than a hundred Zeppelins were used by the Germans during World War I.

BURIAL GROUND

The act of vengeance that created a national shrine.

Montgomery Meigs had reason to be angry at Robert E. Lee. Meigs and Lee had been fellow officers before the Civil War. Both were southerners, West Point graduates, and engineers. They had worked closely together.

But while Lee resigned his commission to lead the armies of the Confederacy, Meigs stayed loyal to the Union, becoming quartermaster general of the Union Army. He watched in anger as Lee's armies filled up Union cemeteries with dead. And every day he could see Lee's prewar mansion mocking him from a hillside high above Washington.

Meigs found the perfect way to punish the Confederate commander. He recommended that Lee's longtime home be turned into a national cemetery.

Meigs wanted to fill the beautiful grounds with Union dead. When bodies weren't buried close enough to the house, he came out to personally supervise the burial of twenty-six soldiers in Mary Lee's beloved rose garden. He wanted bodies to ring the house so that the Lees could never return.

Northerners approved wholeheartedly. One Washington paper thought it "a righteous use of the estate of the rebel General Lee," and by the end of 1864, more than seven thousand soldiers were buried there. Mary

Quartermaster General Montgomery Meigs. His own son is among the Civil War dead buried at Arlington Cemetery, and Meigs himself lies there as well.

Lee was devastated to find that the house was now "surrounded by the graves of those who aided to bring all this ruin on the children and the country."

Today Arlington Cemetery is the closest thing there is to hallowed ground in America. And it might not exist but for a soldier's anger at an old comrade.

Lieutenant John Bailey is one of the soldiers buried in Mary Lee's rose garden, just a few steps from the Lees' home.

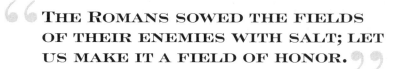

> **THE ROMANS SOWED THE FIELDS OF THEIR ENEMIES WITH SALT; LET US MAKE IT A FIELD OF HONOR.**
>
> —MONTGOMERY MEIGS TO ABRAHAM LINCOLN

A BITTER HARVEST

Did President Lincoln set in motion the events that led to his own assassination?

In 1864 President Lincoln personally approved a daring cavalry raid on Richmond, Virginia. The stated goal was to free Union prisoners held at Richmond's Libby Prison and hand out copies of President Lincoln's amnesty proclamation. The four thousand Union cavalrymen met fierce resistance and got nowhere near Richmond. The mission that started with such high hopes turned out to be a complete fiasco.

Its aftermath proved catastrophic.

During the retreat, an officer commanding one wing of the raid, Colonel Ulric Dahlgren, was shot and killed by Confederates. In his pockets they found papers that suggested the raid had another, far darker, purpose: to kill Confederate president Jefferson Davis and burn Richmond to the ground.

The North denied everything, but southerners were outraged. A Richmond newspaper called it "The Last Raid of the Infernals." The discovery of the documents whipped up tremendous sentiment for taking revenge on the Union.

And so the South unleashed its own covert operations in the North. Numerous plots were hatched by angry conspirators, some with the sanction of the Confederate government, some not. One plot to kidnap President Lincoln and hold him for ransom involved an actor named John Wilkes Booth. When that plan fell apart, Booth began work on another plot—one that would come to fruition the night of April 14 at Ford's Theater.

From a president's order full circle to a president's assassination. A bitter harvest indeed.

> ## THE CITY MUST BE DESTROYED AND JEFF. DAVIS AND CABINET KILLED.

—FROM AN ADDRESS TO HIS TROOPS FOUND IN COLONEL DAHLGREN'S POCKET

Overall command of the raid was held by the man who suggested it: Colonel Judson Kilpatrick, known as "Kill Cavalry" for his reckless style of leadership. His orders for the raid came directly from the president and the Secretary of War.

After Dahlgren's death, arguments erupted over whether the documents found on his body were real or forged. The controversy continues to this day. There is evidence to suggest that the documents may indeed be real, and that the killing of Jefferson Davis was secretly ordered by Secretary of War Edwin Stanton, most likely without Lincoln's knowledge. Stanton was famous for advocating harsh measures against the leaders of the Confederacy.

THE DAY THE IRISH INVADED CANADA

A Fenian fiasco proves the law of unintended consequences.

They came across the border the night of June 1, an army of Irish-American nationalists—Fenians, as they called themselves—ready to fight and die to free Ireland from British rule.

So what they heck were they doing in Canada?

Their goal was to seize the British territory's major cities and use them as bargaining chips to negotiate with Britain for Ireland's independence. Clearer thinkers among them understood this was far-fetched, but they hoped that an invasion launched from American soil would start a war between the U.S. and Britain that would result in British troops being pulled out of Ireland.

And so eight hundred Irish-American soldiers, most of them Civil War veterans, crossed over from Buffalo and invaded Ontario. There was the Thirteenth Tennessee Fenian Regiment, the Seventh New York, the Eighteenth Ohio, and others. They raised the Fenian banner and hoped for the best.

A regiment of Canadian volunteers confronted the Irishmen the next day in the Battle of Ridgeway. It was more of a glorified skirmish, really, which ended when the Fenians routed the Canadian volunteers with a bayonet charge. It would be their first and only victory. When Canadian reinforcements began to appear, the Fenians skedaddled back to the United States, where they were all promptly arrested by U.S. authorities. Another group of

Fenians who crossed over from Vermont into Quebec were similarly unsuccessful.

The bizarre invasion had more impact on Canada than Ireland: it sparked a surge in Canadian nationalism that helped unify the provinces and lead to the creation of the modern Dominion of Canada.

Irish Independence would have to wait another fifty years.

At the Battle of Ridgeway, the Canadian troops suffered ten dead and thirty-eight wounded. The Fenians lost only a handful of men. Colonel John O'Neil, a Civil War cavalry veteran who led the invasion, led two more Fenian invasions of Canada, in 1870 and 1871, each one a more resounding failure than the one before.

CHEW ON THIS

From the Alamo to the invention of modern chewing gum.

A ntonio López de Santa Anna liked to refer to himself as "the Napoleon of the West." Most famous for storming the Alamo in 1836 and putting the defenders to the sword, he became ruler of Mexico four different times before the Mexicans finally drove him into exile.

So it was that Santa Anna became a New Yorker—for a while.

In 1869 the seventy-five-year-old dictator was living on Staten Island. He had in mind a scheme to raise money for another revolution in Mexico by selling chicle, the gummy resin taken from sapodilla trees. Upon meeting an inventor named Thomas Adams, he painted a rosy picture of how they could both make a fortune by turning chicle into a low-priced rubber substitute. Adams agreed to give it a try.

Their get-rich scheme was a complete failure. Adams spent a year experimenting on the chicle, but to no avail. Santa Anna ended up going back to Mexico, and Adams ended up stuck with the useless chicle. He was ready to dump it in the East River when he walked into a drugstore and saw a little girl ordering chewing gum made out of paraffin wax. Remembering that Mexicans chewed chicle, Adams thought he might salvage his stash by turning it into chewing gum.

Chewing chicle proved far superior to chewing wax. "Adams New York Gum Number 1" became hugely popular. It was the first modern gum, the forerunner of every package of chewing gum on store shelves today, and it launched a chewing-gum craze that is still going strong.

One more reason the motto "Remember the Alamo" should *stick* in your mind.

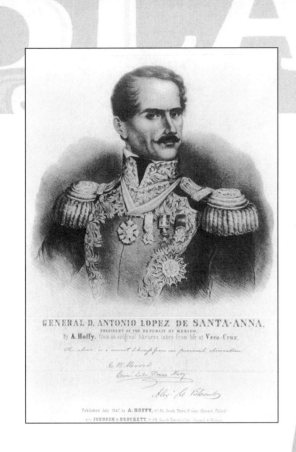

GENERAL D. ANTONIO LOPEZ DE SANTA-ANNA.
PRESIDENT OF THE REPUBLIC OF MEXICO.
By A. Hoffy, from an original likeness taken from life at Vera-Cruz.

Published July 1847, by A. HOFFY, N° 19, South Third Str. abov Chesnut, Philad.ª
also JOHNSON & BROCKETT, N° 24, South Seventh Str. opposit. S. Market.

Mayan Indians started chewing chicle two thousand years ago, and people in Mexico have been doing it ever since. Santa Anna himself probably chewed chicle, which may be how Adams knew he could turn his failed rubber substitute into a new kind of gum.

Adams followed up on his first gum with others, including licorice-flavored "Blackjack," and one product still on the market: Chiclets.

PARIS POST

The birth of air mail . . . more than thirty years before the Wright brothers' first flight.

In 1870 the Prussian army had Paris under siege. The city was surrounded. For five months there was no way in or out. Except by air. In order to keep in touch with the rest of the world, Parisians turned their attentions skyward. Two of the city's railroad stations were turned into balloon factories. Seamen were trained as balloonists. Over the duration of the siege, sixty-four hot-air balloons were produced and launched. Two were lost at sea, and six were captured by the Prussians. But the rest managed to carry more than two million dispatches to the outside world—nearly ten tons of mail.

Alas, the world's first airmail service had one drawback: it went only one way.

They couldn't use balloons to get messages back to Paris, because it is almost impossible to control where a balloon will go. To solve that problem, the balloons leaving the city carried hundreds of carrier pigeons. The birds were taken to various cities, loaded with messages for Paris, and then released. Letters were photographed, reduced in size, and printed on thin films that could hold up to twenty-five hundred messages each. A single pigeon could carry as many as a dozen strips of film with more than thirty thousand dispatches.

The pigeons, however, weren't as reliable as the balloons. Only one in eight made it back. But they carried over a million messages back to the besieged Parisians.

Airmail: a wartime innovation that couldn't wait for the airplane.

At Orléans Station in Paris, more than a hundred women worked to make the balloons. They treated the calico fabric with linseed oil, ironed it, cut the material to precise measurements, then sewed the pieces together by hand.

One balloon leaving the besieged city flew 875 miles and landed in a Norwegian forest.

WINDS OF WAR

The storm that may have prevented a world war.

It began with a civil war in the Pacific island kingdom of Samoa. Germany decided to intervene and put troops ashore to fight for one of the factions. The United States took a dim view of this: German aggression in the Pacific was considered a threat that couldn't be ignored.

Three U.S. warships were dispatched to Samoa to keep an eye on the three German warships already there. Tensions between the two countries grew. Heated messages flashed back and forth between Washington and Berlin. America was angry, Germany defiant.

U.S. public opinion was inflamed by reports that American citizens in Samoa were being ill-treated by German soldiers and that an American flag had been torn down. When a San Francisco newspaper reported (incorrectly) that the Germans had sunk an American ship, conflict seemed imminent. Storm clouds were gathering, figuratively speaking.

Then they started to gather for real.

On March 19, a powerful typhoon struck the island with a force that no one expected. The fierce winds and deadly waves destroyed or severely damaged all six of the U.S. and German warships. Fifty Americans and ninety-five Germans perished in the storm. Many of the rest found themselves dazed and shipwrecked on shore.

But, as the expression goes, it is an ill wind that blows no good. The natural disaster eased tensions at a critical moment, and talk of war took a backseat to planning rescue and recovery efforts. Eventually Germany and

the United States agreed to put Samoa under a joint protectorate. War between the two countries would come, but not for another twenty-five years.

" IN ALL MY EXPERIENCE ON SEA I HAVE NEVER SEEN A STORM EQUAL TO THIS ONE. "

—ADMIRAL LAWRENCE KIMBERLY, COMMANDER OF THE U.S. NAVAL FORCES AT SAMOA

The German ship Adler *was blown completely ashore, although it was later re-floated. Another German ship, the* Eber, *was ripped apart, resulting in the loss of most of its crew. Two American ships, the* Vandalia *and the* Trenton, *sank down to their decks.*

Officers who had been readying for the possibility of a fight found themselves attending memorial services not only for their own dead but for those of their supposed enemy.

One naval cadet serving on the *Vandalia* was commended for his "coolness, zeal and pluck" during the storm. Cadet John Lejeune was eventually commissioned as a Marine Corps officer and was later the thirteenth commandant of Marines. Camp Lejeune in North Carolina is named after him.

FIGHTING JOE

*Whose side was he
on anyway?*

After the sinking of the battleship *Maine* in Havana Harbor, the United States mobilized for war with Spain. Many prominent people clamored for a chance to join the army as high-ranking officers. Assistant Secretary of the Navy Theodore Roosevelt was one. Another was a powerful congressman named Joe Wheeler. President McKinley appointed Wheeler a major general of volunteers. It made perfect sense: Wheeler, after all, had military experience, having served as a general during the Civil War.

Of course, at that time he had been fighting *against* the United States.

"Fighting Joe" Wheeler was a cavalryman who had earned his stars as a major general in the Confederate Army. Now he was trading in the old gray uniform for a new blue one, to serve as a general in the very army he had once considered his a sworn enemy.

Wheeler was a bantam rooster of a man, five foot two and all fight. "A regular gamecock," Theodore Roosevelt called him. Competitive to the core, he exclaimed that he wanted to be the first to encounter "the Yankees . . . damn it, I mean the Spaniards." At times he seemed to think he was fighting the Civil War all over again. "Let's go, boys!" he reportedly cried at the Battle of San Juan Hill. "We've got the damn Yankees on the run again!"

Wheeler's appointment was greeted by many as a sign that the War Between the States was finally a thing of the past and that the nation was whole again.

Wheeler was a Confederate general at age twenty-six and a U.S. Army general at age sixty-one. One of the units he commanded in Cuba was Teddy Roosevelt's Rough Riders.

Wheeler stayed in the army after the war. In 1902, former Confederate general James Longstreet was visiting West Point when he ran into Wheeler in full regalia. Recalling a deceased Confederate comrade, the feisty Jubal Early, Longstreet said: "I hope Almighty God takes me before he does you for I want to be within the gates of hell to hear Jubal Early cuss you in the blue uniform." Wheeler died in 1906 and was buried in Arlington National Cemetery, one of only two former Confederate generals buried there.

A TALE OF TWO GENERALS

Meet the famous general you never heard of.

General Douglas MacArthur was one of the most talented, flamboyant, and controversial men ever to put on a military uniform. His remarkable achievements in World War II and the Korean War have led many to regard him as the greatest military man of all time. And he certainly was a one-of-a-kind figure.

Well, not exactly.

There's another general from an earlier era whose career was remarkably similar. Like Douglas MacArthur, he earned his reputation fighting in the Pacific. Like Douglas MacArthur, he thrilled the nation with his exploits in the Philippines. Like Douglas MacArthur, he rose to become the highest-ranking general in the army. And, like Douglas MacArthur, he was eventually removed by the president for insubordination and brought home, triggering a national controversy.

Both men came within a hairsbreadth of being killed on the battlefield. Both were nominated as young officers for the Congressional Medal of Honor, but didn't actually receive the award until decades later.

Is it just an odd coincidence that Douglas MacArthur's career so closely mirrored the life of this earlier military hero? Just a random happenstance?

Unlikely.

Because that man was General Arthur MacArthur, Douglas MacArthur's father—whose greatest legacy may have been the son who spent a lifetime trying to live up to his old man.

Arthur MacArthur fought in the Civil War, the Indian Wars, and the Spanish-American War, while his son, Douglas, saw action in World War I, World War II, and Korea. Together their careers spanned nearly a century of U.S. military history.

" ARTHUR MACARTHUR WAS THE MOST FLAMBOYANTLY EGOTISTICAL MAN I HAD EVER SEEN . . . UNTIL I MET HIS SON. "

—COLONEL ENOCH CROWDER, AIDE TO GENERAL ARTHUR MACARTHUR

When Douglas MacArthur came ashore during the retaking of the Philippines in 1944, the beachmaster wouldn't let his landing craft tie up at a dock, and he had to wade ashore in his freshly cleaned and ironed uniform. MacArthur was angry, but later, when he saw a photo of it, he realized its great publicity value. The following day he staged another wading ashore for the newsreels.

Neither man's ego was able to handle being subordinate to civilian authority. When President McKinley appointed a civilian governor of the Philippines, Arthur MacArthur, then military governor, accused him of "unconstitutional interference." Douglas MacArthur labeled his own sacking by the president as one of the most "disgraceful plots" in U.S. history.

GLORY DEFERRED

He missed gold by a hair . . . but he would have medals aplenty in the future.

The young military officer had thirsted for glory ever since he was a young boy. After graduating from West Point, he was desperate for some way to prove himself.

One problem: there were no wars going on.

So he turned to a different arena. He traveled to Stockholm to represent the United States at the 1912 Olympics. His event was the Modern Pentathlon, which tested competitors in five military skills: horsemanship, fencing, running, swimming, and shooting.

The young lieutenant performed excellently in every event except the one he considered his best: pistol shooting. Most of his shots punched holes right inside the bull's-eye. But for two of his shots, the judges ruled that he missed the target entirely. The officer himself believed the shots were so good they went through one of the earlier bullet holes.

The gold medal was in the balance. But his argument fell on deaf ears. Instead of finishing first, he finished fifth, his thirst for glory still unquenched.

But don't feel too bad for the failed Olympian. He would find glory more than thirty years later, leading the tanks of the Third Army across what Shakespeare once called "The vasty fields of France," punching holes in the German lines, and making headlines back home. A young lieutenant no more, he would become known as "Old Blood and Guts"—General George S. Patton, finally achieving the fame and plaudits he had sought his entire life.

17592

It was only four years after competing in the 1912 Olympics that young George Patton got a chance to start making his reputation with the newfangled weapon that would one day make his name famous: the tank.

Patton, on the right, took pride in the fact that even though he did not medal in the competition, he came in third in the fencing and gave the French army champion his only defeat.

If scoring had been done in the American manner—ten points for a bull's-eye, nine for the next ring, and so on—Patton's shooting would have placed him third for that event and the overall gold medal would have been his. But the Swedish method counted any hit on a target equally, so his numerous bull's-eyes did him no good, while his alleged misses ruined his score.

THE LAST CHARGE

Remembering the day of days at a place called Gettysburg.

The fateful charge of Pickett's Brigade came on July 3, the third day at Gettysburg. With tens of thousands watching in awe, these brave men set off beneath the fierce afternoon sun. A mile of farm fields separated them from the Union soldiers up on Cemetery Ridge, but come what may, they were intent on coming to grips with their enemy.

Proudly they marched, battle flags waving, a spectacle more dramatic than anyone there had ever seen. As they drew close, the rebel yell broke from their throats.

The Yankees, crouched behind a stone wall, could wait no longer. Hearts about to burst with emotion, they flung themselves forward to meet the enemy.

And then everyone hugged and cried.

Because this was not the Battle of Gettysburg. It was the veterans of Gettysburg, North and South, reenacting the battle fifty years later to the day. The survivors of Pickett's Charge retraced their steps with canes and crutches, as their Union counterparts and more than a hundred thousand spectators looked on. The very men who in their youth had fought as bitter enemies now united to walk the field of battle in peace.

The white-haired veterans, many wearing the same uniforms they had fought in fifty years before, exchanged handshakes where they had once exchanged gunfire. Enemies no more.

> **AS THE REBEL YELL BROKE OUT AFTER A HALF CENTURY OF SILENCE . . . A MOAN, A GIGANTIC SIGH, A GASP OF UNBELIEF ROSE FROM THE ONLOOKERS.**
>
> —PHILIP MEYERS, A SPECTATOR OF THE EVENT

The battlefield became a field of tents as fifty-three thousand Civil War veterans, Union and Confederate, came to the 1913 Grand Reunion at Gettysburg. It's almost the exact same number of men who were killed and wounded in the pivotal Civil War battle.

FLYING CIRCUS

*An aviation first
in the Mexican
Revolution?*

Two primitive biplanes made of wood and cloth approached each other early one November morning. The pilots exchanged a few loosely aimed pistol shots and then roared off in different directions.

It doesn't sound like much, but it may well have been the first aerial dogfight the world had ever seen.

The pilots were American mercenaries who had hired themselves out to competing factions in the Mexican Revolution. Former San Francisco newspaper reporter Phil Rader was flying for General Huerta, while lifelong soldier of fortune Dean Lamb was in the pay of General Carranza. Rader had been dropping primitive bombs on Carranza's forces, and Lamb had gone up to find him.

Years later, Lamb recalled that when the two planes met, Rader fired first. But it appeared to Lamb that Rader was aiming to miss, so he did the same! (Not that they had much chance of hitting each other, anyway, firing pistols from airplanes.) The two pilots gaily emptied their pistols, reloaded, and made another pass. When it was all done they saluted each other and then went their separate ways.

During World War I, when the two men served together, Lamb says they shared a few laughs about the whole affair.

Air combat has become far more deadly in the years since, but it seems to have never completely lost the touch of romance introduced that day in the skies over Mexico.

Dean Ivan Lamb's colorful career also included working on the Panama Canal, serving in Britain's Royal Flying Corps, founding the Honduran Air Force, taking part in several South American revolutions, getting indicted for jewel theft, acting as intelligence officer for the Flying Tigers, and testifying at Alger Hiss's espionage trial. He was an incurable adventurer who once estimated that he served in thirteen different armies.

This is the plane Lamb flew, a Curtis Model D Pusher—a plane that surely did not offer a great deal of protection in aerial combat! To reload his pistol, Lamb had to hold the gun between his knees and put the bullets in with one hand while holding on to the stick with the other.

LIGHTS! CAMERA! WAR!

What happens when a commanding general goes into the movie business?

In January of 1914, Mexican revolutionary Pancho Villa made headlines, not with a battle or a fiery speech, but with something very different: a movie contract.

Villa signed a $25,000 contract with Mutual Films giving them exclusive rights to cover his army. According to its terms, all other cameramen were banned from coming on Villa's campaign, and the general was guaranteed a percentage of the gross.

All that without an agent.

Four cameramen were dispatched to join up with Villa's army. The general obligingly held off an attack on the town of Ojinaga until they got there. He also agreed that if Mutual couldn't get good enough pictures during actual battles, he would stage them.

Mutual decided to make a film about Villa's life, and the general agreed to play himself—even though he was still leading an army in battle! Mutual felt Villa's sloppy old clothes didn't come across well on film, so they gave him a snappy new uniform he was happy to wear. When producers complained that executions at dawn were too hard to film, Villa moved the shootings to later in the day, when there was better light. A location manager's dream.

This is a frame from one of the movies shot of Pancho Villa's army. Soon after Villa signed his contract, another rebel commander signed his own movie deal for exclusive rights to film his branch of the army. War may be hell, but the movie business is really cutthroat.

One journalist called it "the war waged to make a movie." In reality, it was Villa's way of trying to finance his revolution—and generate some good PR. The general was portrayed in Mutual's movies as a hero until his invasion of the U.S. in 1916. After that he became a first-class villain.

That's showbiz.

Mutual Films exec Harry Aitken told the New York Times *that his company had bought ten specially designed cameras to cover the war. The cameras were modified, he said, so that they could film military action without the cameramen being exposed to fire. Here cameraman Charles Rohsher is filming some of Villa's camp followers.*

" HOW WOULD YOU FEEL TO BE A PARTNER TO A MAN ENGAGED IN KILLING PEOPLE? "

—MUTUAL FILMS' HARRY AITKEN, COMMENTING ON THE DEAL

Villa lost most of his support when he invaded the town of Columbus, New Mexico, in 1916, killing seventeen people. His goal was to prompt a U.S. invasion of Mexico that would anger Mexicans and inspire them to flock to his banner. It worked like a charm.

THE BATTLE OF THE LUXURY LINERS

A saga of the high seas with an amazing twist.

There's never been a naval engagement quite like it: two top-of-the-line ocean liners duking it out on the high seas. What made it even stranger was this:

Each ship was disguised as the other.

The *Carmania* was a British ocean liner, the *Cap Trafalgar* a German vessel. At the start of World War I, each ship was commandeered by its respective government and converted into an armed merchant cruiser. Sandbags were stacked up in lieu of armor, and guns bolted to the deck. Two weeks after war was declared, both were ready for military service.

The *Carmania* set out on its first war mission from Liverpool, the *Cap Trafalgar* from Buenos Aires. Each captain knew that his vessel was no match for heavily armored warships, and in the interest of self-preservation, each hit upon the idea of disguising his ship to make it look like an enemy vessel.

Some strange fate must have been at work, because the two captains each decided to disguise his ship as the other. They made the alterations as they sailed on toward a destiny that must have seemed unimaginably improbable.

For as luck would have it, the two vessels happened upon each other off the Caribbean island of Trinidad. Each ship saw through the other's disguise immediately, and the battle commenced. The giant ships dueled for an hour, until the *Carmania* sent the *Cap Trafalgar* to the bottom.

And the battle of the luxury liners was over.

The battle was fought on the numerically satisfying day of 9/14/1914.

The Carmania *had only two funnels, so the crew had to add a dummy third funnel to make it look like the* Cap Trafalgar. *The German ship, meanwhile, dismantled one of its forty-foot funnels and repainted the remaining funnels the same color as the* Carmania*'s.*

CHRISTMAS TRUCE

The day the fighting stopped—and a soccer game broke out.

Christmas Day 1914 saw millions of young men facing each other in a double line of trenches several hundred yards apart that snaked hundreds of miles across Europe. These soldiers had seen some desperate fighting in the opening months of World War I, and plenty more lay ahead.

But on this particular day, peace seemed to break out all over.

In violation of orders, British and German soldiers climbed out of their trenches waving flags of truce and made their way into no-man's-land to celebrate Christmas with their enemies. Leaving the horror of war behind for one day, they shared Christmas pudding and belted out songs together. They exchanged toasts and traded cigarettes and food. "Most peculiar Christmas I've ever spent, and ever likely to" scribbled one British soldier in his diary.

In one place along the line, German soldiers from Saxony were fraternizing with Scottish Highlanders when one of the Scots brought out a soccer ball. A few minutes later a full-fledged game was under way on the frozen turf of no-man's-land. Men who had been trying to kill each other just the day before played enthusiastically for more than an hour.

A German lieutenant, Johannes Niemann, wrote home about the game: "We Germans really roared when a gust of wind revealed that the Scots wore no draw-

Many men took snapshots like this one showing themselves posing with enemy soldiers, and sent them home to their families to prove that it really happened. The Christmas fraternization was quickly condemned by generals, and a number of participants were court-martialed.

ers under their kilts. The game finished with a score of three goals to two in favor of Fritz against Tommy."

The next day, the impromptu truce ended as quickly as it began . . . and the men who had celebrated together returned to the ugly job of killing each other.

One Welsh regiment manning the trenches received a barrel of beer from the Germans facing them as a Christmas present.

The soccer game, of course, had no referee; but the men on both sides took a perverse pride in playing precisely according to the rules.

> ## FANCY A GERMAN SHAKING YOUR FLAPPER . . . AND THEN A FEW DAYS LATER TRYING TO PLUG YOU.
>
> —HERBERT SMITH, FIFTH BATTERY, ROYAL FIELD ARTILLERY

THE BLACK SWALLOW OF DEATH

He was the first African-American military pilot . . . and so much more.

Gene Bullard's last job was working as an elevator operator in New York's RCA Building. He probably had the most amazing résumé of any elevator operator in history.

Born the grandson of a slave in 1894, he stowed away on a ship to Europe when he was just ten. He started prizefighting at age sixteen, and when World War I broke out, he joined the French Foreign Legion. His infantry unit was known as the "Swallows of Death."

Bullard saw two years of action at the front, and was badly wounded at the Battle of Verdun. While recuperating, he volunteered for the French Air Service. In 1917 he became the world's first black combat pilot. Involved in countless air skirmishes, he had one confirmed kill and another unconfirmed one.

After the war he became a well-known character in Paris. He took drumming lessons to get in on the jazz craze, and got a job as a band leader at Zelli's Zig Zag bar in Montmartre. Later he owned a club himself. But his days of military service weren't over.

In 1939, Bullard was recruited to gather information for French intelligence. When the Germans invaded in 1940, he picked up a rifle to fight for his adopted homeland, and was severely wounded. He was smuggled out of Europe and returned to the United States.

Gene Bullard of Columbus, Georgia, won more than fifteen medals for his service to France. In 1954, when the French were relighting the eternal flame at the Tomb of the Unknown Soldier at the Arc de Triomphe in Paris, who did they give that honor to?

An elevator operator from New York.

In 1960 Bullard was made a Chevalier of the French Legion of Honor. His other decorations included the Croix de Guerre, Croix de La France Libre, Medaille Militaire, Cross of the French Flying Corps, Croix de Combattants, Medaille Inter-Alliée, Medaille L'Etoille Rouge, and Medaille de la Victoire.

In his first dogfight, Bullard shot down a German Fokker, then barely made it back to Allied lines before his engine died and he crash-landed. When he got back to base, mechanics counted seventy-eight bullet holes in his Spad airplane.

Bullard saw his whole life as a fight against discrimination. He emblazoned his plane with the motto "Tout le sang qui coule est rouge!" — "All blood runs red." When the United States entered the war in 1917, Bullard tried to join the U.S. Army Air Corps, but was turned down because of his race.

ONE AGAINST WAR

America's most passionate and persistent pacifist.

Jeanette Rankin was the first woman elected to the House of Representatives. A Republican from Montana, she vowed to represent women and children all over the country.

Rankin was sworn in on April 2, 1917. Just four days later, the House faced a historic vote on whether or not to declare war against Germany.

Rankin voted no.

"I want to stand behind my country," she said, "but I cannot vote for war." Her decision resulted in a barrage of criticism. The *New York Times* said it was "final proof of the feminine incapacity for straight reasoning." Rankin was defeated at the next election.

After more than twenty years working as a lobbyist for peace, Rankin was elected to a second term in 1940. After Japan bombed Pearl Harbor, Rankin faced another vote on a declaration of war.

Once again, she voted no. That made her the only member of Congress to vote against war with Japan, and the only one to vote against U.S. entry into both World War I and World War II. "As a woman I can't go to war, and I refuse to send anyone else," she said. Unfriendly epithets rained on her from all quarters. She was called a "skunk," a "traitor," and a "Nazi." Again her vote led to her defeat at the polls.

No one ever called Jeanette Rankin a flip-flopper. In 1968, at the age of eighty-seven, she led a march on Washington to op-

pose what she called the "ruthless slaughter" in Vietnam. At the end of her life she was asked if she would have done anything differently. "Yes," she said. "I would have been nastier."

Miss Jeanette Rankin

Rankin was elected to Congress before women in much of the country could vote. Montana passed a female suffrage law in 1914, but women in most states couldn't vote until ratification of the Nineteenth Amendment, in 1920.

After Rankin's vote against war with Japan in 1941, she was confronted in the halls of Congress by a mob of press, politicians, and angry protestors. She barricaded herself into a phone booth and called Capitol Hill security, who fought their way through the crowd and escorted her safely to her office.

The Rankin campaign of 1917 was an early pioneer in the use of "phone banks" to get out the vote. According to a *New York Times* report the day after the election, "Her friends telephoned to practically everyone in the state who had a telephone . . . and greeted whoever answered the telephone with a cheery 'Good morning. Have you voted for Jeanette Rankin?' "

THE FEMALE LAWRENCE OF ARABIA

The audacious Englishwoman who drew the borders of modern Iraq.

Gertrude Bell was a Victorian woman who did things women just weren't supposed to do. Eschewing the idea of a proper marriage and quiet life in England, she made the Middle East her passion. It was among the Bedouin that she truly felt at home.

In the years before World War I, Bell traveled extensively throughout the Middle East. Crisscrossing the Syrian and Arabian deserts, she developed an encyclopedic knowledge of the tribes and their chieftains, and wrote of her travels in widely acclaimed books.

When war broke out she was recruited by British intelligence to obtain the loyalty of Arab sheiks throughout the Middle East. Bell boldly ventured behind enemy lines to gather information. When T. E. Lawrence set out to spark an Arab revolt, he relied on invaluable research and intelligence supplied by the indefatigable Miss Bell. It was remarked that she was the brains behind Lawrence's brawn.

The headstrong Bell sometimes found herself frozen out by British military officers resentful that a woman was telling them what to do. But her knowledge of the Arab world was too great to ignore. She proved indispensable to military and diplomatic efforts in the Middle East.

After the war, in 1921, British colonial secretary Winston Churchill asked Bell to create the borders of modern Iraq. She pushed to unite Shiites, Sunnis,

and Kurds in one country despite their mutual hostility, thereby setting the scene for much of the turmoil that has since plagued that troubled country.

Gertrude Bell: a woman determined to make her mark in a man's world. Which she undoubtedly did.

Gertrude Bell flanked by Winston Churchill and T. E. Lawrence. For her efforts in World War I, she was honored as a Commander of the British Empire.

Influential sheiks and Islamic leaders, men who never had looked on a woman unveiled, would smoke cigarettes and drink coffee with Bell, seeking her advice or help. She became known as "El Khatun" . . . "The Lady."

> **EVERY ARAB IN THE PENINSULA KNOWS HER. WHEN YOU SPEAK OF 'GERTRUDE,' EVERY ENGLISHMAN FROM CAIRO TO TEHERAN KNOWS WHOM YOU MEAN.**

—*NEW YORK HERALD*, 1926

ENIGMA

How the Poles helped win World War II before it even began.

On a Saturday in January 1929, a crate shipped from Berlin arrived at the customs office in Warsaw, Poland. It was soon followed by a German official explaining that it had been shipped there by accident, and demanding it be returned to Germany *before* going through customs.

This aroused the suspicion of customs officers. Forcing open the crate, they took photos and made diagrams of the odd-looking device inside before returning it to the Germans.

This was Poland's first introduction to the famous Enigma coding machine.

No one had been able to break Germany's Enigma code, but the Poles were determined to try. A team of brilliant young cryptographers, led by Marian Rejewski, attacked Enigma with innovative mathematical techniques. By 1932 they had built a working model of the machine and were decoding German military messages. But it was a constant struggle for code breakers to keep up.

In 1938 the Germans created a new and improved Enigma machine. The Poles could no longer decipher German messages. Knowing that war was on the way, they shared their information with the French and British, just weeks before the Germans invaded.

It was a priceless gift.

The Poles were decades ahead of other countries in breaking Enigma. Their efforts paved the way for the now famous code-breaking effort that eventually allowed the Allies to read the Germans' most secret messages, which proved instrumental in winning the war.

An Enigma machine in the command vehicle of German general Heinz Guderian. The Germans believed Enigma was unbreakable, and trusted their most important messages to it.

The role played by the massive Allied decipherment project wasn't revealed until 1974. One of those most surprised was Marian Rejewski, who never knew until then just how critical his prewar code-breaking efforts were to eventual Allied victory.

" UNE MOMENT DE STUPEUR. "

—A FRENCH INTELLIGENCE OFFICER, DESCRIBING THE MOMENT THAT THE POLES UNVEILED THEIR RE-CONSTRUCTED ENIGMA MACHINES TO THE ALLIES IN JULY OF 1939.

The Poles gave their reconstructed Enigma machines to France and Britain. One of the machines was smuggled to London in the baggage of playwright Sacha Guitry and his wife, actress Yvonne Printemps, so as not to raise the suspicion of German spies. Two weeks later, Germany invaded Poland.

THE GOOD MAN OF NANKING

*The Nazi business-
man who became a
savior for thousands.*

Japanese forces sweeping through China reached the capital city of
Nanking on December 13, 1937. After taking control, they began to execute Chinese POWs. The killing quickly spiraled out of control. Men were
rounded up for bayonet practice. Women were raped by the tens of thousands. People were beheaded for sport. Snapshots taken by Japanese soldiers
captured the frenzy of violence known to history as the Rape of Nanking.

A surprising hero emerged during this reign of terror: an unassuming German businessman named John Rabe.

The small group of westerners still in Nanking created a "Safety Zone," hoping to make it a safe haven for refugees of war. They elected Rabe their leader
in the belief that his Nazi Party membership would afford him influence with
the Japanese.

Desperate Chinese began to flood the Safety Zone to escape the massacre.
When Japanese soldiers pursued them even there, Rabe assumed the role of

protector. He fearlessly confronted Japanese commanders, demanding that they control their soldiers. He threw his own
property open to refugees. He began patrolling the Safety Zone
himself, pulling Japanese soldiers off of rape victims, and chas-
ing them away without weapons. His only defense: an armband
sporting a Nazi swastika. "They don't want to tangle with a German," he wrote in his diary. "Usually all I have to do is shout
'Deutsch' and 'Hitler' and they turn polite."

Japanese troops went on an eight-week orgy of murder and violence in Nanking, killing an estimated three hundred thousand men, women, and children in what some have called the forgotten holocaust. But more than two hundred fifty thousand crowded into the Safety Zone were spared . . . thanks in no small part to a good man named John Rabe.

To this day, the Japanese government and Japanese textbooks downplay the Rape of Nanking, saying that the death toll has been greatly exaggerated.

Rabe, in center, with other members of the Safety Committee. After returning to Germany, Rabe wrote a letter to Hitler about the atrocities in Nanking, expecting the Führer to be outraged over his Japanese allies. Instead he was arrested by the Gestapo and ordered never to speak about his experiences in China. "I don't think he thought so much of Hitler after that," said his granddaughter, Ursula Reinhardt.

> **YOU HEAR OF NOTHING BUT RAPE. IF HUSBANDS OR BROTHERS INTERVENE, THEY'RE SHOT.**
>
> —JOHN RABE

THE RESCUER

*Fate offered him
a second chance
. . . and he took it.*

It's called the Miracle of Dunkirk. In May of 1940, German forces advancing through France were on the verge of capturing an entire Allied army. Nearly surrounded, British and French soldiers fought their way to the coastal town of Dunkirk in a desperate bid to escape.

The British Admiralty put out the call for every small craft it could find to help stage an emergency evacuation. Yachts, fishing boats, motor launches, tugboats, any vessel that could pull men off the beaches. Despite constant attack by German bombers, this motley fleet managed to rescue more than three hundred thousand men and bring them back to England. Winston Churchill called it a "miracle of deliverance."

One of the legion of heroic rescuers was a sixty-six-year-old retiree named Charles Lightoller. Determined to bring home every man he could, he crammed more than 120 soldiers on his small motor yacht. Then he piloted the dangerously overloaded vessel back across the English Channel, dodging bombs and bullets all the way.

Perhaps his zeal to rescue as many men as possible was driven in part by memories of a harrowing night at sea nearly thirty years before. It was a night be could never forget: lifeboats being launched only half full . . . cries of distress in the water . . . despair at not being able to do more. An April night in 1912 when more than nine hundred people perished in the icy North Atlantic, despite the best efforts of Charles Lightoller.

Second officer on the RMS *Titanic*.

The evacuation effort was called Operation Dynamo. At the start, no one expected that more than a handful of soldiers could be saved—but over ten days, 338,000 men were rescued so they could fight again.

THE MAN WHO SAVED BUCKINGHAM PALACE

A royal rescue of the first order.

The air-raid sirens sounded at nine-thirty that Sunday morning. As Big Ben struck noon, the skies over London began filling up with warplanes.

It was September 15, now remembered as the fiercest day of the Battle of Britain. More than four hundred German bombers attacked London. Adolf Hitler was determined to destroy Britain's will to fight, and Buckingham Palace was a prime target. The official residence of the royal family had been hit twice in recent days, suffering minor damage. It seemed only a matter of time before it suffered a direct hit.

RAF fighter pilots battled desperately all day to protect the city. Toward the end of the battle, Sergeant Ray Holmes shot down one bomber and then saw another German plane making an unobstructed run straight toward the palace. Holmes was out of ammunition. But he didn't hesitate.

He flew his Hurricane fighter directly into the German plane, slicing off its tail and sending it hurtling to the ground below. Then he managed to parachute out of his own plane before it crashed on Buckingham Palace Road.

Street crews later paved over the remnants of Holmes's plane, which remained buried for more than sixty years, until archaeologists recovered the

engine and some other parts in 2004. The dig was broadcast live on television. Eighty-nine-year-old Ray Holmes looked on with interest.

"What goes through a young pilot's mind as he confronts the Germans?" he was asked. "Nothing particularly," answered the man who saved the palace. "Except he just has to go and have a bash at him. That's all."

King George VI and his wife, Queen Elizabeth, viewing bomb damage to Buckingham Palace. "I'm almost glad we've been bombed," said the queen. "Now I can look the East End in the face."

Starting in August of 1940, German bombers attacked Britain for eighty-four straight days. They failed to break the British spirit and lost an estimated 2,765 planes in the process. "Never in the field of human conflict was so much owed by so many to so few" said Winston Churchill in praise of the RAF pilots who ultimately repulsed the German attack.

THE LADY IS A SPY

1940

From banana dancer to decorated hero.

Josephine Baker was a dancer, a singer, and a daring sex symbol. She was also a highly successful intelligence operative. The American-born Baker came to Paris in the 1920s, and her provocative dancing took the town by storm. In 1940, when war broke out, she offered her services to the French Resistance. "France has made me what I am," she told a Free French leader. "Parisians have given me everything, especially their hearts. Now I will give them mine."

One of her superiors was skeptical: "I was afraid she was one of those shallow show-business personalities who would shatter like glass if exposed to danger." But she proved cool as a cucumber.

Josephine Baker

When the Germans invaded Paris, she let members of the Resistance hide out in her remote château. Dispatched to neutral Lisbon to establish contact with the Free French, she set up concerts as a cover story, and carried vital information written with invisible ink on her sheet music. "The destiny of the Free French," said her boss, Colonel Paolle, "was written in part on the pages of 'Two Loves Have I.' "

Invited to diplomatic parties, she acted the part of a ditzy dancer, and then wrote down everything she heard. "My notes would have been compromising if discovered," she said later, "but who would dare search Josephine Baker to the skin."

After the war Charles de Gaulle awarded her the Légion d'Honneur and the Medaille de la Résistance for her efforts. When she died, the sensation who had once shocked Paris with her banana dance became the only woman ever to receive a twenty-one-gun salute in France.

Baker joined the Follies Bergere in 1926. Just twenty years old, she became one of the highest-paid performers in France. Her famous banana dance, performed topless in a skirt of rhinestone-studded bananas, drove audiences crazy.

The citation on Baker's Légion d'Honneur noted that she possessed "un sang-froid remarquable."

C'EST UNE FEMME COURAGEUSE.

—DANIEL MAOURANI, LE DEUXIEME BUREAU, THE FRENCH EQUIVALENT OF THE CIA

HEROES O'HARE

Chicago's O'Hare Airport is named after a hero. But which one?

Butch O'Hare was America's first flying ace of World War II. On February 20, 1942, he spotted a formation of Japanese bombers preparing to attack the carrier USS *Lexington* in the waters off New Guinea. Diving into their midst, he shot down six of them single-handedly, saving the ship and the lives of thousands aboard. This action won him the Congressional Medal of Honor.

Butch died in combat the following year. In 1949 the citizens of Chicago honored Butch O'Hare by naming their airport after him.

That's not all there is to the story, however.

Butch's father was a lawyer and racetrack owner named Eddie O'Hare. "Artful Eddie," as he was known, got involved with Chicago mob boss Al Capone in the 1920s. That connection made him a ton of money, but he was worried about the impact on his teenage son. O'Hare was dead set on his Butch getting into the U.S. Naval Academy, and he figured he would have to break away from Capone before that could happen.

So "Artful Eddie" cut a deal with the feds. For the sake of his son's future, he volunteered to risk his life and inform on Capone. He detailed the mobster's operations for IRS agents, and led them to a bookkeeper who could testify about Capone's illegal income. As a result, prosecutors were able to convict Capone on charges of tax evasion and send him to prison in 1931. Butch O'Hare got an appointment to the Naval Academy a year later.

So while O'Hare Airport bears the name of a World War II hero, it also commemorates a father willing to do anything for his son, and the man who helped prosecutors win their war against Al Capone.

" **ONE OF THE MOST DARING, IF NOT THE MOST DARING, SINGLE ACTION IN THE HISTORY OF COMBAT AVIATION.** "

—FRANKLIN D. ROOSEVELT, AWARDING BUTCH O'HARE THE CONGRESSIONAL MEDAL OF HONOR

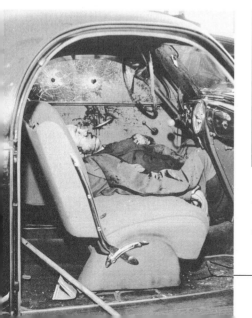

Eddie O'Hare also played a critical role in the trial of Capone. He revealed to prosecutors that the fix was in—that Capone's henchmen had bribed or coerced everyone in the jury pool. Acting on that information, Judge James Wilkerson switched jury panels with another judge on the first day of the trial. The jury selected from that panel went on to convict Capone and send him to Alcatraz.

Eddie O'Hare paid the ultimate price for informing on Capone. In 1939, shortly before Capone was released from prison, he was gunned down on the orders of Chicago gangster Frank Nitti.

GADZOOKS!

Jazz, the Marines, radio, and the weapon that helped win World War II.

Sergeant Bob Burns was a championship rifleman in the Marine Corps during World War I. But as good a marksman as he was, he was a better musician. Burns organized a Marine Corps Jazz Band that was a favorite of General John Pershing and played to troops across Europe.

Burns was especially well known for playing an instrument that he invented himself. It was made out of two pieces of gas pipe and a whiskey funnel. It was sort of a combination of a trombone and a slide whistle, and it became Burns's trademark. He even coined a funny name for it.

After World War I, Burns became a radio entertainer and a movie star. He was known around the country as the "Arkansas Traveler," casting himself as a homespun rube telling tales of the Ozarks. But the cornerstone of his success was that wacky instrument of his. In the late 1930s and early '40s, at the height of his popularity, thousands of toy versions were manufactured and sold to kids across America.

Burns's instrument is forgotten today, but the name he dreamed up for it lives on—with a very different meaning.

In the early days of World War II the army was testing a new shoulder-mounted antitank gun called the M1A1 at the Aberdeen Proving Ground. The soldiers trying it out thought that it bore a remarkable resemblance to the odd contraption Burns had made famous. And so it got the nickname by which it is still remembered.

The bazooka.

TO PLAY HIS BAZOOKA HERE

Jazz Band Sergeant Introduces New Gas Pipe Tone-Teaser.

Sergeant Robert Burns, who organized General Pershing's Jazz Band during the war, has introduced a new musical instrument for dance music here. Burns has just arrived from London with his unique instrument, which he calls the bazooka. It has much the same tone as a deep-toned saxaphone, and consists of two pieces of gaspipe, to which are attached funnellike ends.

The instrument is the result of Burns's ingenuity during the war, when musical instruments of all kinds were so greatly needed and the crude material was all

The United States
manufactured nearly half a million bazookas
during World War II, along with 15 million of the antitank rockets
it fired. The bazooka proved so successful at stopping enemy tanks
that the Germans copied it outright. They did, however, give it another name, calling it the Panzerschreck, or "tank terror."

Burns's bazooka sounded like a
low-toned saxophone with a range
of about six notes. Burns was
equally adept at playing the instrument for laughs or turning in virtu-
oso jazz performances with it.

Where did Burns get the name? He said once
that he took it from the now-obsolete slang
word "bazoo," meaning mouth, as in "he blows his
bazoo" (he talks too much). He told other people
that the name mimicked the sound the strange instrument made.

AN OFFER HE COULDN'T REFUSE

How a notorious mobster played a part in America's war effort.

War can make for some strange bedfellows. None stranger, perhaps, than when U.S. Naval Intelligence hooked up with the Mafia during World War II.

It began when the SS *Normandie*, a former French ocean liner being converted into a troop ship, rolled over and burned at its New York City moorings in February of 1942. The navy thought it might be sabotage. Concerned about dockside security, and always looking for ways to gather information, Naval Intelligence decided to seek help from New York's most powerful mobster:

Charles "Lucky" Luciano.

Luciano was serving a thirty-year jail term, but he agreed to cooperate. He "encouraged" his gangland associates to work with the navy. Mob capos passed the word to hundreds of dockworkers and fishermen that they should report any suspicious activity . . . or else. When the U.S. was getting ready to invade Sicily, Luciano put them in touch with people who had connections to the Sicilian underworld.

After the war, the navy tried to cover up its wartime marriage to the mob. All records were destroyed, and the navy officially denied that they had gotten much in the way of substantial help from Luciano. To this day it is unclear exactly how useful he was.

But consider this: despite a huge public outcry, Luciano was released from

prison and deported to Sicily less than six months after the war was over, though he was years away from completing his sentence. A reward, perhaps, to a man whose contribution the government could never afford to officially recognize.

Luciano volunteered to parachute into Sicily in order to gather information prior to the Allied invasion. The navy turned him down.

> **THE GREATER PART OF THE INTELLI-GENCE DEVELOPED IN THE SICILIAN CAMPAIGN WAS . . . FROM THE CHARLIE 'LUCKY' CONTACT.**

—LIEUTENANT COMMANDER CHARLES HAFFENDEN, NAVAL INTELLIGENCE, AFTER THE WAR (HE WAS LATER DISCIPLINED BY THE NAVY FOR MAKING THOSE COMMENTS)

Late in life, Luciano claimed that he had ordered his men to set the fire that sunk the Normandie, as a way of shaking down the navy. But the elderly Luciano was famous for making wildly exaggerated claims about his earlier days, and a navy investigation showed no evidence of sabotage.

A parade of big-name mobsters got into the act. Meyer Lansky (seen here), Bugsy Siegel, and Frank Costello were all involved in gathering information for the navy. Lansky in particular hated Hitler for his actions against European Jews.

THE YOUNGEST HERO

A boy determined to do a man's job.

In August of 1942, Calvin Graham walked into a recruiting station in Fort Worth, Texas. He was shipped out to the Pacific, where he joined the crew of the USS *South Dakota* as a gunner.

It wasn't long before Graham found himself in harm's way. First came the Battle of Santa Cruz in October. Two weeks later it was the Battle of Guadalcanal, in which the battleship took forty-seven hits in a desperate night action. Graham was knocked down a stairway by an explosion that peppered his jaw with shrapnel. Though seriously wounded, he worked through the night, fighting fires and pulling fellow crewmen to safety.

And how did the navy reward Calvin Graham's heroism in battle? They shipped him stateside, put him in the brig for three months, stripped him of his veteran's benefits, and gave him a dishonorable discharge. It seems that after the battle, Graham carelessly let slip that he had lied on his enlistment papers. Specifically, he had lied about his age.

Calvin Graham was twelve years old.

He is believed to be the youngest of the thousands of underage servicemen who fought for the United States in World War II.

The navy didn't quite know what to do with Graham. Eventually his sister got him sprung by threatening to go to the papers. Two days after his thirteenth birthday, he rejoined his Fort Worth classmates in the seventh grade—undoubtedly the only veteran in the group.

Graham's gunnery officer on the South Dakota (and the man to whom he admitted his true age) was Sargent Shriver, who later married JFK's sister, Eunice Kennedy, headed the Peace Corps, and ran for president in 1976.

Calvin Graham joined the navy to flee a broken home and an abusive stepfather. He said the recruiting officer knew he was underage but had no idea that he was only twelve. A navy dentist who noticed his twelve-year molars weren't in tried to have him discharged, but Graham managed to slip his file into the "approved" pile when the dentist wasn't looking.

Graham never stopped fighting to have his navy service recognized. In 1978, President Jimmy Carter ordered the navy to grant him an honorable discharge. And in 1994, the navy finally agreed to give him a Purple Heart for his injuries suffered off Guadalcanal. Graham didn't live to see it, having died two years before.

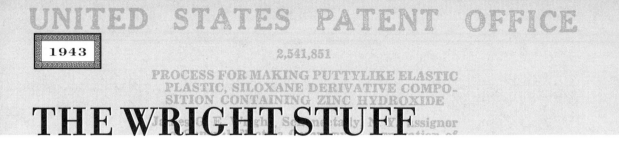

UNITED STATES PATENT OFFICE

1943

2,541,851

PROCESS FOR MAKING PUTTYLIKE ELASTIC
PLASTIC, SILOXANE DERIVATIVE COMPO-
SITION CONTAINING ZINC HYDROXIDE

THE WRIGHT STUFF

A wartime shortage that led to something silly.

During World War II, Japanese armies in the Far East cut off America's access to its rubber supply. The country faced a shortage so severe that the government implemented gasoline rationing, even though there was plenty of gas, in order to conserve the rubber used in car tires.

Scientists got busy searching for a synthetic rubber substitute. At General Electric, engineer James Wright tried to find a way to make a rubber-like substance out of silicone. One day in 1943 he poured boric acid into a test tube filled with silicone oil, hoping they would combine to make hard rubber. Instead, the mixture turned into a soft, gooey putty. Pulling some out of the test tube, he dropped it on the table.

It bounced.

GE sent samples of the new substance to scientists around the world to see if anyone could figure out a use for the stuff. Nobody could, although they certainly enjoyed playing with it. The new substance was put on the shelf as a failure.

In 1950, a marketing consultant in Connecticut named Peter Hodgson got his hands on some of the stuff from a chemist friend and saw a gold mine in it. He knew right away that while scientists might regard it as useless, kids would love it. He packed the putty into plastic eggs and gave it a name we all know today:

Silly Putty.

t is particularly concerned with novel composi-
ions which because of their unusual properties
nay best be described as "bouncing putties."   5

The invention is based on the discovery that
ompositions possessing a unique combination of
roperties including both a high degree of elas-
icity or "bounce" under suddenly applied stresses
nd a high degree of plasti... ...a stress is   10
pplied more slowly... ...ting
dimethyl silicone...

ture of 100 to 150 degrees C. for 2 hours. The
final product can be worked between the fingers
in the same manner as ordinary window putty,
and the more it is worked the more putty-like it
becomes. The product also exhibits a high degree of elasticity or bounce.

The use of a hydrolyzable alkyl borate or equivalent catalyst provides a convenient way of obtaining a thorough dispersion of the boron compound in the methyl silicone oil. The following

More than 300 million eggs containing 4,500 tons of silly putty have been sold since 1950. On its fiftieth birthday, in 2000, Silly Putty was enshrined in the Smithsonian Institution, right next to the hula-hoop.

Patented Feb. 13, 1951   2,541,851

UNITED STATES PATENT OFFICE

2,541,851

PROCESS FOR MAKING PUTTYLIKE ELASTIC PLASTIC, SILOXANE DERIVATIVE COMPOSITION CONTAINING ZINC HYDROXIDE

James G. E. Wright, Schenectady, N. Y., assignor to General Electric Company, a corporation of New York

No Drawing. Application December 23, 1944, Serial No. 569,647

2 Claims. (Cl. 260—37)

1

The present invention relates to novel compositions of matter comprising a dimethyl silicone. It is particularly concerned with novel compositions which because of their unusual properties may best be described as "bouncing putties."

The invention is based on the discovery that compositions possessing a unique combination of properties including both a high degree of elasticity or "bounce" under suddenly applied stresses and a high degree of plasticity when the stress is applied more slowly, can be obtained by treating a dimethyl silicone with a compound of boron, preferably followed by a further treatment of the product with heat, a catalyst, or both. By the term "dimethyl silicone," as used herein, and in the appended claims, is meant the oily methyl polysiloxanes obtained by hydrolysis of a pure or substantially pure dimethyl silicon dihalide or equivalent hydrolyzable dimethyl silicon com-

2

then added, worked into the mass, and the resultant product heated in an oven at a temperature of 100 to 150 degrees C. for 2 hours. The final product can be worked between the fingers in the same manner as ordinary window putty, and the more it is worked the more putty-like it becomes. The product also exhibits a high degree of elasticity or bounce.

The use of a hydrolyzable alkyl borate or equivalent catalyst provides a convenient way of obtaining a thorough dispersion of the boron compound in the methyl silicone oil. The following example illustrates the preparation of a plastic, elastic composition by use of an ester of boric acid:

Example 2

A mixture of 200 parts of dimethyl silicone oil, 22.5 ethyl borate and 2.3 parts ferric chloride hexahydrate is placed in a suitable container and steam introduced into the mixture for one-half hour in order to hydrolyze the ester. The re-

BORMAN LOVELL ANDERS

Numerous newspapers, magazines, and websites claim that the astronauts of Apollo 8 took Silly Putty to the moon, and used it to alleviate boredom and affix tools to the walls of the spacecraft. Sad to say, that's an urban myth. NASA, the makers of Silly Putty, and Apollo 8 astronaut Jim Lovell all say it's not true.

PIGEONS IN A PELICAN

*The weapons
system controlled
by a birdbrain.*

During World War II, the U.S. Navy began work on a rocket-propelled guided missile, but prototypes of the so-called "Pelican" missile were not performing up to expectations. Then stepped forward a scientist who had an unusual idea for how to steer the missile to its target.

A pigeon would control the guidance system.

Famed behaviorist B. F. Skinner believed he could use positive reinforcement to train the pigeons to guide missiles to the target—although the outcome might not be too positive for the bird. He convinced the Pentagon to provide funding for the idea.

Thus began "Project Pigeon."

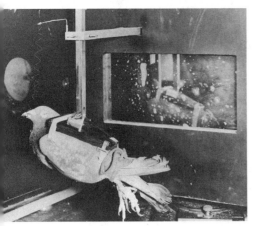

A lens and mirror system projected an image of the distant target on a screen directly in front of the pigeon. The bird was trained to peck at the target, activating a mechanism that would turn the missile in that direction.

As outlandish as that might sound, Skinner and his team succeeded in training the pigeons and building a prototype homing device. They were able to demonstrate that it was both highly effective and easy to manufacture. But in the end, the pigeons never got off the ground. Neither scientists nor generals were able to take the project seriously enough to actually put the homing device in a missile and test it.

And so it was that a missile with a birdbrain was shot down for good.

Skinner never lost enthusiasm for Project Pigeon. Fifteen years after the war, he was still defending it, suggesting that pigeons could guide a rocket to the moon.

The propotype of the missile nose cone held three pigeons—redundant guidance systems, just like NASA would later use in the space program.

The "Pelican" was more a radio-controlled rocket plane than it was a guided missile. It never saw action, but its development led to the "Bat" guided missile (no bats were involved) which was used to sink several Japanese ships in the closing days of the war.

ONE-SIDED BATTLE

The consequences

of fighting blind.

In 1942, the Japanese invaded and occupied the Aleutian islands of Attu and Kiska. It was the first time American soil had been occupied by an enemy since the War of 1812, and the United States was determined to throw them out.

The Americans retook the island of Attu in May of 1943, suffering heavy casualties. Then, in August, came the invasion of Kiska.

A joint American-Canadian force of thirty-five thousand hit the beaches, backed up by a massive naval fleet. The initial landings were unopposed, but the soldiers knew from experience that the Japanese would want to lure them in before answering their fire. The battle soon turned into a nightmare. Heavy gunfire could be heard, but thick fog made it impossible to see the enemy. Reports of casualties started filtering in, and wounded men were taken to the rear. Soldiers moved slowly forward, clambering up tough mountain ridges, firing as they went.

After two days of heavy fighting, with thirty-two soldiers dead and more than fifty wounded, the Allies made a stunning discovery:

There was no enemy.

The Japanese, it turned out, had staged a cunning evacuation three weeks before, pulling six thousand men off the island without American blockaders even having a clue. The battle deaths were all from friendly fire. Americans and Canadians had fought with great bravery. But, as it turned out, they were shooting at each other.

The invasion, code-named Cottage, was later referred to by Time magazine as a JANFU: Joint Army Navy Foul-Up.

> ## SURPRISE WAS ACHIEVED, BUT IT WAS NOT THE JAPANESE WHO WERE SURPRISED.

—ARMY REPORT ON THE BATTLE

All the Japanese occupiers had left behind was one dog, who was quite delighted to defect to the American side.

A COUNRTY OF HEROES

How the citizens of tiny Denmark stood up to Adolf Hitler.

In September of 1943, Adolf Hitler signed an order for Denmark's Jewish population, as yet largely untouched by the Holocaust, to be deported to the death camps.

Nazi officials planned to begin the roundup on the night of October 1. More than a thousand German police and Gestapo officers came to Denmark to handle the action. Ships and trains were readied to whisk the Jews away.

The response of the citizens of Denmark deserves to be remembered for all time.

The Danish government, tipped off about the roundup, warned Jewish families to go into hiding. Many non-Jewish Danes risked their lives to hide and protect their Jewish neighbors. That led to a spontaneous nationwide effort to smuggle Denmark's Jews to safety in Sweden—"a conspiracy of decency," one author has called it. Haphazard at first, the rescue mission soon became an organized effort of the Danish underground. Churches and hospitals were used as gathering points. Universities closed down for a week—and students worked side by side with resistance fighters to get the Jews secretly to the coast.

From there, more than three hundred fishing boats ferried Denmark's Jews to Sweden, which welcomed them with open arms. More than 90 percent of Denmark's seven thousand Jews managed to escape the German sweep.

There was no one hero. There was a country of heroes. Which is why Israel's Holocaust memorial Yad Vashem honors the entire Danish people as "Righteous Among Nations" for risking the wrath of Germany to help their Jewish countrymen in their hour of need.

It is worth noting that Denmark's Jews might never have been saved but for a German diplomat, George Duckwitz, who tipped off the Danish government to the impending roundup. And many German military officers in Denmark—perhaps seeing which way the war was going—turned a blind eye to what was going on.

The crossing to Sweden was not free—Danish fishermen demanded steep fees for the potentially dangerous passage. But many Danes opened their purses to total strangers so that no family would be unable to cross for lack of funds.

When the Swedish government publicly offered Danish Jews asylum, an official German communiqué referred to the Swedes as "Swine in dinner jackets."

THE GREATEST HOAX IN HISTORY

To make the invasion of Normandy a success required deception on a grand scale.

I n the spring of 1944, Allied commander Dwight Eisenhower gave General George Patton a mighty army to spearhead the invasion of France. The First U.S. Army Group consisted of eleven divisions assembled near the White Cliffs of Dover, readying to cross the English Channel at its narrowest point and invade France at Pas-de-Calais.

But it wasn't a real army—it was a giant con job.

The Allies wanted to convince Hitler that the planned invasion was just a diversion, that the real invasion was going to come more than one hundred miles away, near Cherbourg. So began Operation Quicksilver.

Set designers from London's famous Shepperton Studios were brought in to create the illusion of a massive army where there was none. They created battalions of rubber tanks, and regiments of wooden soldiers. Canvas airplanes were parked on fake runways, harbors filled with dummy landing craft. Radio operators sent huge amounts of bogus traffic, orders to and from units that didn't exist.

A professor of architecture from Britain's Royal Academy used broken sewage pipes and rusty old oil tanks to create a fake refinery. Movie studio wind machines blew clouds of dust over the scene, making it look as if construction was proceeding at a furious rate.

The deceptions fooled Hitler completely. Even after the Allies stormed ashore in Normandy on June 6, the Germans held their Panzer divisions in reserve, waiting for a phantom invasion from a ghost army that was purely the product of Allied imagination. That gave the Allies the time they needed to secure the beachhead and make possible the triumph of D-Day.

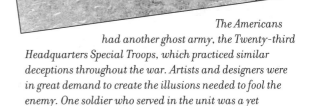

The Americans had another ghost army, the Twenty-third Headquarters Special Troops, which practiced similar deceptions throughout the war. Artists and designers were in great demand to create the illusions needed to fool the enemy. One soldier who served in the unit was a yet unknown fashion designer named Bill Blass.

General Patton was discouraged not to be leading the real invasion, but he warmed to his role as commander of a nonexistent army, racing around the south of England making fighting speeches and maintaining a high profile. "I'm a natural-born ham," he said.

Numerous other ruses were also employed to mislead the Germans. Actor M. E. Clifton-James, seen here, impersonated British general Bernard Montgomery, and traveled to Gibraltar and Algiers shortly before D-Day to convince Germans that something was cooking there.

IS PARIS BURNING?

Paris on the eve of destruction . . . and the only man who can save the city has orders to destroy it.

Allied armies were rolling through France in August of 1944, but Adolf Hitler was determined they would never get to Paris. He handpicked General Dietrich von Choltitz to take command of the city. Von Choltitz was a hero of the Russian front, but he had never had an assignment like this one. "I received orders," he said, "to turn Paris into a mass of ruins and to fight and die amidst its wreckage."

Von Choltitz prepared to do his duty. He ordered explosives planted in landmarks such as Notre-Dame Cathedral and Les Invalides. He told his superiors that he was ready to blow up the Arc de Triomphe and the Eiffel Tower.

Hitler had chosen von Choltitz because of his unswerving loyalty. But the monocled general was troubled by his orders. He couldn't bear to go down in history as the man who destroyed Paris.

So he made a decision that could have earned him an execution. As pressure grew on him to begin destruction of the city, he secretly agreed to a truce with the Resistance, and got a message to the Allies begging them to invade . . . but quickly. They needed to enter Paris within forty-eight hours; otherwise, he would be forced to carry out his orders.

The Allies had been planning to bypass Paris, but when General Omar Bradley got the message, he acted fast. "Have the French Division hurry the hell in there," he ordered.

In his Berlin bunker, Hitler screamed: "Is Paris burning?" But thanks to von Choltitz . . . the City of Light was saved.

Von Choltitz surrendered the city after a brief fight, forgoing the destructive house-to-house battle that Hitler had ordered. The German High Command considered von Choltitz a traitor, and he was ostracized by fellow German veterans after the war.

As he awaited the Allies, von Choltitz feared he would be deprived of his command for disobeying destruction orders. But the German ambassador, Otto Abetz, agreed to help by sending a telegram to Berlin protesting von Choltitz's "brutality." That convinced Berlin he was being tough, and bought him the extra few days he needed.

Though Hitler's armies conquered Paris and occupied it for more than fifteen hundred days, the Führer himself spent only a few hours there in June 1940, and never returned.

❝ **PARIS MUST NOT FALL INTO THE HANDS OF THE ENEMY, OR IF IT DOES, HE MUST FIND THERE NOTHING BUT A FIELD OF RUINS.** ❞

—HITLER'S ORDERS TO VON CHOLTITZ, AUGUST 23, 1944

PATTON'S PRAYER

Everybody talks about the weather, but one general decided to take action.

In December of 1944, General George Patton's Third Army found itself bogged down in Belgium. The Germans were only part of the problem. Patton's army was also hampered by terrible weather: rain, fog, and floods were making advance nearly impossible.

Not content to sit idly by, Patton abruptly summoned one of his officers and told him what he wanted:

A prayer for good weather.

The officer he called on was Third Army chaplain James O'Neill. "I'm tired of having to fight mud and floods as well as Germans," Patton told him. "See if we can't get God to work on our side." O'Neill got right to work. The prayer he wrote beseeched the Almighty to "restrain these immoderate rains" and "grant us fair weather for battle."

When he brought it back to Patton, the general told him he wanted 250,000 copies printed up. "We've got to get every man in the Third Army to pray," Patton said. The soldiers received the prayer card on December 22, the very day they were supposed to launch a desperate counterattack in the Battle of the Bulge. As if by magic, the rain and fog disappeared. Six days of perfect weather followed, during which the Third Army handed the Germans a crushing defeat.

Patton called O'Neill into his office. "Chaplain, you're the most popular man in this headquarters. You sure stand in good with the Lord and the soldiers." Then he pinned a Bronze Star on O'Neill . . . a medal for a prayer that worked wonders.

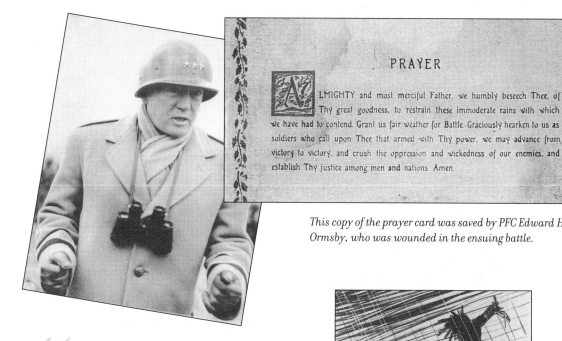

PRAYER

ALMIGHTY and most merciful Father, we humbly beseech Thee, of Thy great goodness, to restrain these immoderate rains with which we have had to contend. Grant us fair weather for Battle. Graciously hearken to us as soldiers who call upon Thee that armed with Thy power, we may advance from victory to victory, and crush the oppression and wickedness of our enemies, and establish Thy justice among men and nations. Amen.

This copy of the prayer card was saved by PFC Edward H. Ormsby, who was wounded in the ensuing battle.

" WE MUST ASK GOD TO STOP THESE RAINS! "

—GENERAL GEORGE
S. PATTON

FU-GO ATTACK

The intercontinental weapons used to attack America.

Four months after the Japanese attack on Pearl Harbor, sixteen bombers took off from the deck of the aircraft carrier *Hornet* to conduct a daring bombing raid on Tokyo.

While the attack did little damage, it was a psychological blow. Eager to strike back, Japanese war planners searched for a way to hit the American mainland. After two years of intensive top-secret preparation, Japan unleashed the world's first intercontinental weapon on the United States in 1944:

Bomb-carrying balloons.

It may sound funny, but it was anything but. Over a period of months, the Japanese launched more than six thousand of the so-called "Fu-Go" weapons against the United States. The balloons were designed to catch the jet stream for a quick crossing of the Pacific, then drop down on America's cities, forests, and farmlands. Each one carried four incendiary bombs for starting fires, and a shrapnel bomb for sowing terror.

An estimated one thousand of the balloons came down in the U.S. Some reached as far as Michigan, but most came down in the Pacific Northwest. One killed six picnickers in Oregon, while another temporarily shut down a plant in Hanford, Washington, that was part of the atomic bomb project.

The damage was minimal, but the threat was real. The government's response was to censor all news of the attacks. This "de-

fense of silence" convinced the Japanese High Command that the program was a failure, and they discontinued it before their new weapon of terror could reach its full potential.

The spherical balloons were thirty-three feet across. Because of the high winds in the jet stream, the journey across the Pacific took only about four days.

The three hundred–pound payload included navigation instruments, fuse mechanism, and incendiary bombs, three of which can be seen hanging from the bottom ring.

❝WINDSHIP WEAPON❞

—TRANSLATION OF FU-GO, THE NAME
GIVEN TO THE BALLOON BOMBS

Had the Japanese continued the program in the spring and summer of 1945, the balloons would have hit the U.S. at the height of forest-fire season, with a potential for creating chaos in the western states. But the news blackout succeeded in ending the program prematurely.

FLAG DAY

Second time's the charm.

AP photographer Joe Rosenthal was having a bad day. Coming ashore on Iwo Jima to cover the fighting there, he slipped on a ladder and fell from the boat into the ocean. Once ashore, he heard about a flag-raising on Mount Suribachi—a great opportunity for a picture—but was frustrated to learn he was probably too late to catch it.

Still, he joined some soldiers hiking up the mountain. They came under heavy fire. When they were halfway up, soldiers coming down brought Rosenthal the disappointing news that the flag was already up. He thought about heading back, but decided to keep going. Good call.

At the top, he saw that a flag had already been raised. But he also saw a group of Marines getting ready to raise another flag. It turned out that a Marine colonel had ordered a second flag-raising so that the first flag could be kept for posterity.

Rosenthal almost missed the shot. He was trying to get his bulky camera set up on a pile of rocks as the flag started going up, and he wasn't even looking in the viewfinder when he pressed the button. He had no idea if he had snapped a decent picture. When the film was developed, it turned out that frames 9 and 11 were ruined by light leaks.

But frame 10, the picture snapped that day, turned out bold and beautiful. "Here's one for all time," said the photo editor who first saw it. Printed on front pages across the country, it won a Pulitzer Prize and soon became one of the most famous war photographs in history.

Not bad for a bad day.

The six men who raised the flag were Ira Hayes, Frank Sousley, Harlan Block, Michael Strank, John Bradley, and Rene Gagnon. Three of them, Sousley, Block, and Strank, were killed within days.

This was the first flag-raising, photographed by Marine Corps staff sergeant Louis Lowery. This flag was carefully preserved, but the second flag, the one in the famous photo, flew for three weeks, until winds chewed it up. No one thought to save it—it was just the replacement flag, after all.

The Battle of Iwo Jima claimed the lives of 6,821 American soldiers.

SHADES OF GRAY

A wartime replace-ment who was an inspiration to millions.

On Sunday, May 20, 1945, the St. Louis Browns trounced the New York Yankees in both games of a doubleheader. Browns outfielder Pete Gray was the star of the day. In the first game he had three hits, driving in two runs and scoring a third. In the second game he scored the go-ahead run, and made a spectacular catch in the outfield.

Pretty spectacular for a guy with one arm.

During World War II, large numbers of baseball players joined the military, so teams had to look for replacements. One of those called up was Pete Gray.

When Gray was six, he fell off a farm wagon and his right arm got caught in the spokes. It had to be amputated at the elbow. A natural right-hander, Gray learned to throw and bat using only his left hand. His passion for baseball led him to spend untold hours perfecting a way to catch a ball, tuck his glove under his stump, then roll the ball across his chest to his throwing hand in one quick motion.

Eventually he quit school to pursue a baseball career. He joined the pennant-contending St. Louis team in 1945 after a stellar year in the minors, where he batted .333 and hit 6 home runs. His major league numbers were nowhere near as strong—he played in only 77 games and batted .211. When the year was out, and the regulars returned, he was gone from the majors for good.

But to many he was a hero. Pete Gray: a man unwilling to let adversity get in the way of a dream.

Pete Gray

Gray was asked how good he might have been if he had never lost his arm. "Who knows?" he said. "Maybe I wouldn't have done as well. I probably wouldn't have been as determined."

Newspaper reporters referred to Gray as "Wonder Boy." Some of Gray's teammates resented him because they thought he was signed as a gimmick, to put fans in the seats.

OURSE OF CONVE...
ATIVE LATTER REQUIRE THE...
FRENCH TROOPS IN HANOI STOP MEANWHILE FRENC...
...PREPARATIONS FOR A COUP DE MAIN IN HANOI A...
...THEREFORE MOST EARNESTLY APPEAL TO YO...
...WERE URGENTLY IN SUPP...
...N KEEPI...

1945

ABOUT FACE

Imagine saving the life of an ally . . . who winds up becoming your bitterest foe.

In 1945, an American intelligence team code-named "Deer" parachuted into the jungles of Asia to help a band of guerrillas fighting the Japanese. They found the leader of the guerrillas, Nguyen Ai Quoc, seriously ill from malaria and dysentery. "This man doesn't have long for this world," exclaimed the team medic, but he successfully nursed him back to health. The grateful leader agreed to provide intelligence and rescue downed American pilots in return for ammunition and weapons.

The team suggested that the U.S. continue to support Nguyen after the war, but the recommendation was considered too controversial, and it was ignored. The following year, the guerrilla leader pleaded with President Truman to support his movement to gain independence from the French, but the U.S. government decided they didn't like his politics.

Nguyen Ai Quoc was also known by another name: "He Who Enlightens." In Vietamese: Ho Chi Minh. Sixty thousand Americans died in the Vietnam War, battling a former ally whose life the U.S. once fought to save.

In the 1920s, Ho worked as a busboy at the Parker House Hotel in Boston. By 1954 he had become president of an independent North Vietnam. By the 1960s, the onetime U.S. ally was America's Public Enemy No. 1.

Ho Chi Minh (third from right) with members of the OSS "Deer" team that saved his life. In the white suit at left is Vo Nguyen Giap, who later became Ho's military commander and masterminded military efforts against French and U.S. forces.

VIỆT-NAM DÂN CHỦ CỘNG HÒA

CHÍNH PHỦ LÂM THỜI

BO NGOAI GIAO

*

HANOI FEBRUARY 28 1946

TELEGRAM

PRESIDENT HOCHIMINH VIETNAM DEMOCRATIC REPUBLIC HANOI
TO THE PRESIDENT OF THE UNITED STATES OF AMERICA WASHINGTON D.C.

ON BEHALF OF VIETNAM GOVERNMENT AND PEOPLE I BEG TO INFORM YOU
THAT IN COURSE OF CONVERSATIONS BETWEEN VIETNAM GOVERNMENT AND FRENCH
REPRESENTATIVES THE LATTER REQUIRE THE SECESSION OF COCHINCHINA AND THE
RETURN OF FRENCH TROOPS IN HANOI STOP MEANWHILE FRENCH POPULATION AND
TROOPS ARE MAKING ACTIVE PREPARATIONS FOR A COUP DE MAIN IN HANOI AND
FOR MILITARY AGGRESSION STOP I THEREFORE MOST EARNESTLY APPEAL TO YOU
PERSONALLY AND TO THE AMERICAN PEOPLE TO INTERFERE URGENTLY IN SUPPORT
OF OUR INDEPENDENCE AND HELP MAKING THE NEGOTIATIONS MORE IN KEEPING WITH
THE PRINCIPLES OF THE ATLANTIC AND SAN FRANCISCO CHARTERS
RESPECTFULLY

HOCHIMINH

FLOOR IT

The wartime shortage that turned leftovers into legend.

In the days following World War II, good lumber was in short supply and usually had a high price attached to it. So when Anthony DiNatale got an order in 1946 for a large wooden floor, to be built at the lowest possible cost, he had to use some imagination. He located some scraps of wood left over from the construction of army barracks. Although it was sturdy hardwood from Tennessee, all the pieces were short.

The workmen at DiNatale Flooring in Boston then fitted the scraps together in an alternating pattern, and constructed a series of five-foot-square panels that could be bolted together to form the entire floor.

In doing so, they constructed what may be the single most famous floor in the world—in the sports world, that is.

It became known the world over as the famous parquet floor of Boston Garden. The floor on which the Boston Celtics won an unsurpassed sixteen championships. A floor unlike that of any other basketball court on earth, trod by the likes of Bill Russell, Bob Cousy, Larry Bird, and Kevin McHale.

DiNatale charged the Celtics $11,000 for the now famous floor. After it was replaced by a new parquet floor in 1999, autographed pieces of the original sold for as much as $300,000 each. A few pieces of the old floor were integrated into the new one to keep the memory of the old floor alive.

The 264 pieces of the floor were fitted together with 988 bolts. The Boston Garden "bull gang" could assemble the floor and lay it down for a game in two and a half hours.

Fans and players alike have speculated that the Celtics had a special home advantage on the parquet because they knew where it's "dead spots" were. But Celtic great Bob Cousy says flatly: "The idea of dead spots is pure, unadulterated crap."

BOMBS AWAY!

*A nuclear nightmare
that was all too close
to coming true.*

Just after midnight, on January 24, 1961, the U.S. Air Force dropped two nuclear bombs on Goldsboro, North Carolina. It was an accident, of course. A fuel leak aboard a Strategic Air Command B-52 Stratofortress caused an explosion that ripped the bombs from the plane and sent them hurtling toward earth. The plane itself crashed shortly thereafter.

One bomb parachuted to earth with little damage. The other slammed into a farmer's field. Neither exploded.

The Defense Department announced at the time that the bombs were not armed and were in no danger of exploding. But later evidence suggested that the truth was far more chilling.

It was subsequently discovered that the bombs had partially armed themselves on the way down, the force of the fuel-leak explosion having triggered the arming mechanisms—all but one, that is. Detonation required the bombs to go through a sequence of six steps, and these bombs went through all but the last. Only a single switch prevented them from detonating.

The Stockholm International Peace Research Institute concluded this may have been the closest the world has ever come to an accidental nuclear catastrophe.

Air force officers trying to find the bombs in the wreckage from the crash told one reporter they were looking for an ejection seat. Portions of one bomb still remain buried in a boggy farm field today. The air force has an easement on the land to prevent anyone from digging deeper than five feet into it.

An atomic bomb accidentally dropped off the coast of Georgia in 1947 is still there, believed to be buried in ten to fifteen feet of mud. The air force says there is no danger of it going off because it doesn't contain the plutonium capsule needed to detonate it.

The MK 39 bombs dropped on Goldsboro were each more than 250 times as powerful as the bomb that destroyed Hiroshima. President Kennedy, who had been in office just four days when this accident occurred, ordered more elaborate arming mechanisms to be installed on nuclear weapons to prevent accidental detonation.

G.I. JOE

The story of an American fighting man.

The president of the Hasbro toy company wanted to make a splash at the 1964 New York Toy Fair. The question was: Which product to go with? It was a choice between a miniature grocery store . . . and a doll for boys.

Hasbro president Merrill Hassenfeld decided to go with the doll.

Of course no one wanted to call it a *doll*. What red-blooded American boy would play with dolls? So the design team coined a new phrase for their product, calling it an "action figure," and put it into production.

That's how it came about that G.I. Joe reported for duty on February 9, 1964. His body was inspired by a twelve-inch-tall wooden sculptor's mannequin that could bend at every joint. His face had a scar on the right cheek so that he looked tougher than Barbie's boyfriend, Ken. (It also made him easier to copyright!)

The U.S. was still mourning President Kennedy's death, the Beatles were taking the country by storm, and Vietnam was not yet part of the national consciousness. G.I. Joe was the right toy at the right time. Soon an army of Joes began to invade American homes.

Joe was retired in 1978, a victim of disillusionment over Vietnam and the OPEC oil embargo, which sent the price of plastic through the roof. A three-and-three-quarter-inch Joe came out in the 1980s, but the original foot-high soldier didn't return to active duty until his thirtieth anniversary, in 1994. He's been going strong since. Sales skyrocketed after 9/11, and it looks like this is one soldier with a long career ahead of him.

Hasbro announced that the face of G.I. Joe was a composite of twenty Medal of Honor winners, but that was just a marketing ploy. Sculptor Phil Kraczhowski, paid $600 to sculpt Joe's head, was instructed to make him a rugged American male. Kraczhowski had done numerous busts of JFK, and many on the design team felt that he incorporated a lot of the president's features in Joe's face.

The unwitting catalyst for the creation of G.I. Joe was TV producer Gene Roddenberry. The man who would go on to create *Star Trek* was producing a TV show called *The Lieutenant*. Marketing consultant Stan Weston approached Hasbro with the idea of creating some kind of toy to tie in with the show. The tie-in idea eventually died, as did the series, but G.I. Joe was on his way. Weston was offered $100,000 in cash or 1 percent of sales. He took the cash, thus losing out on more than $20 million worth of royalties.

ACOUSTIC KITTY

High-tech cats fight the Cold War.

In the 1960s, the Cold War pitted intelligence agents of East against West—CIA versus KGB—in a high-stakes game of espionage cat and mouse. Then somebody decided that an actual cat might be an effective weapon.

Recently declassified documents show that during the sixties, the CIA's Directorate of Science and Technology tried to turn cats into bugs—walking eavesdropping devices for listening in on Soviet diplomats in public places. Project "Acoustic Kitty" reportedly involved five years of design and the expenditure of millions of dollars.

Miniaturized transmitting devices were surgically implanted inside a cat. "They slit the cat open," says one former CIA operative, "put batteries in him, wired him up. The tail was used as an antenna."

Problems were many. The CIA apparently discovered what cat owners have always known: cats are hard to train. They tended to walk off the job when they got hungry or distracted, which was distressingly often. Still, the CIA persisted. One document, parts of which are still classified, praises the patience of those who worked with the feisty felines: "The work done on this projects over the years reflects great credit on the personnel who guided it."

When the wired-up cat was deemed ready for a full-scale test, it was taken to a park and let out of a van. Then disaster struck—in the form of a taxi, which promptly ran over the feline operative. "There they were," said the former agent, "sitting in the van with all those dials, and the cat was dead."

And so was Project Acoustic Kitty.

The idea of a chicken-powered nuke sounds fanciful, but British scientists in the 1960s proposed using chickens as a heating device inside a nuclear landmine. The bomb was designed to be left in the path of attacking Soviet troops, and one top-secret report suggested that enclosing a live chicken inside (with some food) would provide enough body heat to keep the delicate triggering mechanism from freezing in winter weather.

Another animal almost drafted for service in the Cold War was the gerbil. The furry creatures can smell fear—or, more accurately, the increased adrenaline in a fearful person's sweat. Spy-catchers in various countries considered using them in the 1970s. But when airport-security experts in Israel put them to work, they found that the fur-balls couldn't tell the difference between a wrongdoer scared of being caught and a passenger afraid of flying.

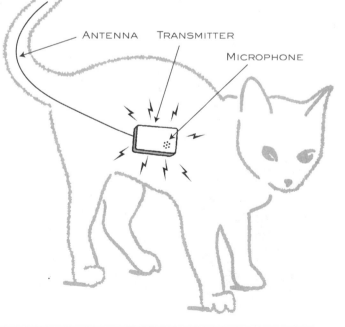

ANTENNA   TRANSMITTER

MICROPHONE

THE SOCCER WAR

We've all heard of tough matches, but a soccer game that started a war?

In June 1969, Honduras and El Salvador faced off in a soccer game, the first in a series of qualifying matches for the World Cup. The two countries were bitter rivals, and the fans in Honduras made sure the visiting Salvadoran team wouldn't be able to sleep the night before the game by setting off firecrackers and honking horns outside their hotel. Not surprisingly, Honduras won 1–0.

Fans in El Salvador were beside themselves. Eighteen-year-old Amelia Bolanios was so distraught she shot herself after Honduras scored the winning goal. Her death was mourned as a national tragedy. "The young girl could not bear to see her fatherland brought to its knees," wrote the Salvadoran newspaper *El Nacional.* An army honor guard led her funeral procession, and the president of El Salvador walked behind the casket.

With emotions running high, the Honduran team came to El Salvador for a second match a few weeks later. Salvadoran troops and tanks ringed the field. After El Salvador won, 3–0, vicious riots broke out among the fans, and several people were killed.

It wasn't only in the stadium that things got out of hand. The game's outcome pushed a century-old border dispute to the boiling point, and war broke out on July 14. Although the fighting lasted only a hundred hours before a cease-fire was agreed upon, casualties were significant: five thousand people were killed and more than ten thousand wounded.

It became known as "La Guerra del Fútbol": The Soccer War. It started on the playing field and ended up on the battlefield.

The war took a terrible toll on noncombatants. Here Honduran refugees flee after two days of Salvadoran artillery attacks.

Salvadoran soldiers poised for action near the Honduras border, one day into the four-day war. It wasn't until 1980 that Honduras and El Salvador finally ironed out their border issues and signed a peace treaty.

One reason many people have never heard of this war is that world attention was focused a quarter of a million miles away that week: on the Apollo 11 lunar-landing mission, which put Neil Armstrong and Buzz Aldrin on the moon July 20, 1969.

LIKE FATHER, LIKE SON

*A tour of duty with
an unusual twist.*

During World War II, Mike Novosel flew a B-29 and participated in the firebombing of Tokyo. At age forty-two, with three children, he found himself so inspired by President Kennedy that he volunteered to fly helicopters for the army in the Vietnam War.

He thought he would be used as an instructor, but instead found himself shipped off to combat, flying in the company of pilots half his age. Eventually he served two tours as a "Dustoff" medevac pilot in Vietnam, airlifting wounded soldiers from the battlefield. He flew more than two thousand missions and evacuated more than five thousand wounded. One particularly dangerous mission earned him a Medal of Honor.

His son, Mike Novosel, Jr., graduated from Army Flight School twenty-seven years to the day after his father. The year was 1969, and he asked to be assigned to his dad's unit, the Eighty-second Medical Detachment. "At the time I just wanted my dad to be proud of me," says Mike Jr. But it was the first and only time in U.S. history that a father and son ever flew together in the same combat unit. And each would have the chance to save the other's life.

When Mike Jr.'s helicopter was forced down by enemy fire, his father flew to the scene and rescued him. Less than seven days later, Mike Jr. rescued his father under similar circumstances.

In 1971, Mike Sr. was awarded the Medal of Honor by President Nixon, who told father and son that they wouldn't be going back to Vietnam. "The Novosels have done enough," he said.

Mike Novosel, Sr., was a lieutenant colonel in the Air Force Reserve when he decided to return to active duty. The air force told him they didn't need him, so he walked away from his officer status and joined the army to fly as a noncommissioned "warrant officer."

During the thirteen-hour mission that won Mike Novosel, Sr., his Medal of Honor, he braved heavy fire to rescue a group of wounded South Vietnamese soldiers. Novosel was credited with saving the lives of twenty-nine men, himself sustaining shrapnel wounds in both legs in the action.

SCRAP METAL WAR

The scrap operation that triggered quite a scrap.

Britain calls them the Falklands. Argentina knows them as Las Malvinas. In 1982 the centuries-old dispute between the two countries over the remote South Atlantic islands was heating up. Argentina's ruling junta hoped to regain control of the British-occupied islands to help restore its fading popularity. But the possibility of war still seemed distant.

Then a wealthy Buenos Aires scrap dealer named Constantino Davidoff sent a group of workmen to salvage scrap metal from an abandoned whaling station on one of the southernmost of the contested islands. He had a contract with the owner and permission from the British embassy to be there.

But when Davidoff's men raised an Argentine flag on the island, it caught the attention of scientists from the British Arctic Survey Team. They reported to British authorities that there had been an Argentine landing.

The British, suspicious that something was up, sent a note of protest to Argentina, and dispatched the warship *Endurance* to watch over the scrap dealers. Argentina sent a warship of its own. The British landed marines. The Argentines sent more ships.

Perhaps this was just the pretext Argentina was looking for. Perhaps it inflamed passions beyond the point of no return. In any case, less than a week later, Argentina invaded the islands.

The salvage operation was over. The war was on.

Britain eventually retook the islands, at a cost of 256 men killed.

Nearly seven hundred Argentine troops were killed in the war. They are the only Argentines who have been allowed to stay on the windswept islands, which are still the subject of bitter disagreement between the two nations.

> ## IF I HAD NEVER BEEN BORN, ARGENTINA AND GREAT BRITAIN WOULD NOT BE FIGHTING.
>
> —CONSTANTINO DAVIDOFF, SIX WEEKS INTO THE WAR

The junta saw the invasion as a way to appeal to patriotic pride and distract people's attention away from 600 percent inflation and other economic problems. They did not expect the British would be willing or able to conduct a major military effort eight thousand miles from London, over a group of windswept islands inhabited by only two thousand people.

The most well-known warrior in the British invasion force was HRH Prince Andrew, son of Queen Elizabeth II, brother of Prince Charles, and known to his fellow helicopter pilots simply as "H."

THE DOMINO'S THEORY

An epic story of War and Pizza.

At five A.M. on Wednesday, January 16, 1991, the word flashed out from Washington: war with Iraq was imminent, likely to begin within hours. Sure enough, later that day, the bombs began to fall. The Persian Gulf War was under way.

The early warning came not from a high-placed presidential aide or a ranking military officer, but from a more unlikely source: A pizza man.

Frank Meeks owned sixty Domino's pizza franchises in the D.C. area. Meeks was famous for keeping a close eye on pizza orders, and the night before the war began he noticed a sharp uptick in the number of late-night pizza orders coming from the White House, the Pentagon, and the State Department. White House pizza orders went through the roof, with more than fifty pies ordered between ten P.M. and two A.M.

Meeks had seen the same thing happen the night before the invasions of Grenada and Panama. He was sure this meant war, so he called the news media and put out the word. The rest is pizza history.

Will this slice of history prove the ultimate undoing of the republic? Is fast food the soft underbelly of American military might? Will foreign agents start infiltrating Washington pizza joints to see what's baking in government offices? Are counterintelligence agents ready to swing into action with a "Pizza Interdiction Effort" (PIE) to order up a little Domino's deception?

Deliver us.

Pizza prognosticators please take note: according to the Domino's Pizza Team Washington Pizza Meter, the top pizza ordered by the White House in 2003 was a veggie, while the number-one pizza at the Pentagon was a pepperoni.

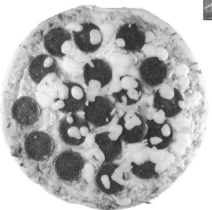

According to one expert, the moral of the story is this: When the going gets tough, the tough get pizza.

"I DON'T THINK THEY'RE SITTING AROUND WATCHING REDSKINS RERUNS."

—FRANK MEEKS, ANALYZING A SURGE IN LATE-NIGHT PIZZA ORDERS FROM THE PENTAGON

SOURCES

"Where do you find these stories" people often ask, and the answer is: "Everywhere." Stories that I first saw online, heard from a friend, found in an old library book, are all here. The trick isn't finding stories, it's verifying them. Sometimes it's easy. Other times it involves hours of research.

I relied primarily on scholarly books, magazine articles, old newspapers, and a small number of websites that demonstrated a scholarly approach and/or a particular expertise with the material. There are several online sources that I consulted so constantly that I have chosen not to cite them every time. The *Encyclopaedia Britannica* (www.britannica.com) is a wonderful source for basic historical information. A sometimes useful variation on that is the 1911 edition of the *Britannica* (www.1911encylopedia.com) with its lengthy in-depth articles on subjects often overlooked today.

For more recent stories, the *New York Times* archive, available to me (with my library card) through the Minuteman Library Network (http://www.mln.lib.ma.us/) allows word searching of stories going back to 1857. The *Time* magazine archive (www.time.com) allows word searching of articles back to 1923. These both offer an opportunity to go back many decades and see how a particular person or event was viewed at the time.

I make no claims to this being a scholarly work. But even in a "popular" work of history, readers deserve to know the principal sources of the information, and where to go to find out more.

The Sacred Band: *100 Decisive Battles* by Paul K. Davis. *Soul of the Sword* by Robert L. O'Connell. *Plutarch's Lives*, translated by John Dryden.

Archimedes' Secret Weapon: *Dio's Roman History (volume II: Fragments of Books XII–XXV)*, translated by E. Cary. *Universal History* by Polybius. (These works excerpted online at http://www.mcs.drexel.edu). *Buffon* by Otis E. Fellows and Stephen F. Milliken. "Archimedes' Mirrors: Some New Reflections," by Malcolm Browne, *New York Times*, March 11, 1978.

Up Against the Wall: *Rubicon* by Tom Holland. *100 Decisive Battles* by Paul K. Davis.

Warrior Princess: *Gladiatrix* by Amy Xoll. "The Celtic War Queen Who Challenged Rome," by Margaret Donsbach, *Military History*, online archive (http://www.thehistorynet.com/mh/blceltic_war_queen).

Daring Dancer: *Condemned to Repeat It* by Wick Allison et al. *Procopius, History of the Wars (volume I)*, translated by H. B. Dewing, excerpted online at the *Internet Medieval Sourcebook* (http://www.fordham.edu/halsall/sbook.html). *The Crusades* by Antony Bridges.

An Islamic Europe?: *100 Decisive Battles* by Paul K. Davis. *Encyclopedia of Events That Changed the World* by Robert Ingpen and Philip Wilkinson.

Spoils of War: *Tilt* by Nicholas Shrady. *Through My Eye: 91st Infantry Division in the Italian Campaign, 1942–45* by Leon Weckstein.

History's Hitmen: *The Assassins, A Radical Sect in Islam* by Bernard Lewis. *The Crusades* by Antony Bridges.

The Swallows of Volohai: *The Mongols* by David Morgan. *The Mongol Empire: Genghis Khan: His Triumph and His Legacy* by Peter Ludwig Brent. *Encyclopedia of Events That Changed the World by* Robert Ingpen and Philip Wilkinson.

Divine Wind: *Storm from the East: From Genghis Khan to Kublai Khan* by Robert Marshall. *The Divine Wind: Japan's Kamikaze Force in World War* II by Captain Rikihei Inoguchi and Commander Tadashi Nakajima.

Arms Race: "Chinese Bombard" by John H. Lienhard, in *Engines of Our Ingenuity* (http://www.uh.edu/engines/epi1744.htm). "The Oldest Representation of a Bombard" by G-d Lu, J. Needham, and C-h Phan, *Technology and Culture*, vol. 29, no. 3, 1988, pp. 594–605. *Gunpowder: Alchemy. Bombards, and Pyrotechnics* by Jack Kelly.

Dangerous Games: *Golf: A Pictorial History* by Henry Cotton. *The Sackville Illustrated Dictionary of Golf* by Alan Booth and Michael Hobbs. "The Perfect Substitute for War," by Paul Auster, *New York Times Magazine*, April 18, 1999.

God Is in the Details: *100 Decisive Battles* by Paul K. Davis. *Encyclopedia of Events That Changed the World* by Robert Ingpen and Philip Wilkinson.

Weapons Wizard: *The Inventions of Leonardo da Vinci* by Margaret Cooper. *Leonardo, the First Scientist* by Michael White.

Siege of Bread and Butter: "A Loaf of Bread: Price and Value" by John Pearn, M.D., *Asia Pacific Journal of Clinical Nutrition* (1998) 7(1):8–14.

Fighting Turtles: *New History of Korea* by Ki-bai Lee. *The Reader's Companion to Military History*, edited by Robert Cowley and Geoffrey Parker. "Admiral Yi Sun-Shin," by Alan Burse, *Korea Herald*, March 19 1997.

A Falling-Out in Prague: *Fighting Words: From War, Rebellion, and Other Combative Capers* by Christine Ammer. "The Empire Strikes Out," *New York Times*, April 18, 1999. *Leonardo's Mountain of Clams and the Diet of Worms* by Stephen Jay Gould. Visit by the author to Hradcany Castle in Prague, August 2004.

Drebbel's Dream: *Submarines and Deep Sea Vehicles* by Jeffrey Tall. *The Navy Times Book of Submarines: A Political, Social, and Military History* by Brayton Harris. "The Saga of the Submarine," by Brett McLaughlin, *All Hands Magazine*, September 1967.

Bees in Battle: "Bees in Warfare," by John T. Ambrose, *Gleanings in Bee Culture*, November 1973. "Bees Go to War," by Roger Morse, *Gleanings in Bee Culture*, October 1955. "War and Bees: Military Applications of Apiculture," by Conrad Bérubé (http://www.apiculture.com).

The Siege That Gave Birth to the Croissant: *A History of Food* by Maguelonne Touissant-Samat. *Reader's Digest Facts and Fallacies.*

The War of Jenkins' Ear: "Earmarked for War," by Jack Rudolph, *American History Illustrated*, February 1984. *A Brief History of the Caribbean* by Jan Rogozinski.

A Dandy Tale: *America's Song: The Story of Yankee Doodle* by Stuart Murray. "Yankee Doodle," Library of Congress website (http://lcweb2.loc.gov/ammem/today/apr19.html).

Old Man's Fight: *Paul Revere's Ride* by David Hackett Fischer.

Fighting Words: *Fighting Words: From War, Rebellion, and Other Combative Capers* by Christine Ammer.

The General's Gambit: *The George Washington Papers at the Library of Congress, 1741–1799* (http://lcweb2.loc.gov/ammem/gwhtml/gwhome.html). *Gunpowder: Alchemy. Bombards, and Pyrotechnics* by Jack Kelly.

Forgotten Fight: *The Battle for New York* by Barnett Schecter. "The True Story of Nathan ('The Torch') Hale: No Wonder They Hanged Him," by Thomas Fleming, *New York Magazine* July 14, 1975.

Miracle at Saratoga: *Saratoga* by Richard M. Ketchum. "Benedict Arnold, Hero: A Revolutionary Turning Point," by R. W. Apple, *New York Times Magazine*, April 18, 1999.

Trick or Treason?: *Unsolved Mysteries of History: An Eye-opening Investigation into the Most Baffling Events of All Time* by Paul Aron. *The Life of Daniel Boone* by Lyman Copeland Draper. "Daniel Boone," by Carole D. Bos, *Lawbuzz.com* (http://www.lawbuzz.com/famous_trials/daniel_boone/daniel_boone.htm).

Bulldog of the Black Sea: *John Paul Jones: Sailor, Hero, Father of the American Navy* by Evan Thomas.

Revolutionary Pencil: *"Get It on Paper,"* THE HISTORY CHANNEL® documentary written and produced by Kate Raisz; Rick Beyer, executive producer. *The Pencil* by Henry Petroski.

America's Worst General: *Duel* by Thomas Fleming. *The War of 1812* by Donald R. Hickey. *Harper Encyclopedia of Military Biography.* "General Wilkinson's Forbidden Realms," by Dianna Serra Cary, *Wild West Magazine*, February 1999.

Blind Man's Bluff: *Fighting Words: From War, Rebellion, and Other Combative Capers* by Christine Ammer. *Horatio Lord Nelson* by Brian Lavery.

The Fever Factor: *Jefferson's Great Gamble* by Charles Cerami. "Insects, Disease, and Military History: The Napoleonic Campaigns and Historical Perception," by Robert K. D. Peterson, *American Entomologist.* 41:147–60.

Shell Shock: *Harper Encyclopedia of Military Biography.* "Honour for the Man Who Changed the Face of War," by June Southworth, *London Daily Mail,* July 28, 1994. "General Henry Shrapnell," *Freshford.com* (http://www.freshford.com/shrapnell).

Rum Rebellion: *Captain William Bligh* by Philip Weate and Caroline Graham. *The Bounty: The True Story of the Mutiny on the Bounty* by Caroline Alexander. Merriam-Webster's *Webster's New Biographical Dictionary,* 1995.

The War of Bad Timing: *The War of 1812* by Donald R. Hickey.

An Army of Two: "Along the South Shore" by S.G.W. Benjamin, *Harper's Monthly Magazine,* June 1878, vol. 57, no.337. *To the Point: The Story of Cedar Point Light* by David Ball. Interview with David Ball, president, Scituate Historical Society, December 9, 2004, along with various documents supplied by the society.

Star-Spangled Banner: Various documents and clippings from National Museum of American History.

Bad Day at Waterloo: *A Brief History of Disease, Science, and Medicine* by Michael Kennedy. *An Underground Education* by Richard Zacks.

Spearheading a Revolution: *The Washing of the Spears* by Donald R. Morris. "Shaka: Africa's Black Napoleon," by Truman R. Strobridge *Military History,* online archive (http://www.thehistorynet.com/mh/blafricasnapoleon).

Budding Statesman: *Encylopaedia Britannica.* Merriam-Webster's *Webster's New Biographical Dictionary.* "The Paul Ecke Ranch Story," Ecke Ranch website (http://ecke.com/new1/corp_story/corp_story.asp).

Davy's Death: *Unsolved Mysteries of American History* by Paul Aron. *How Did Davy Die?* by Dan Kilgore.

Tea Party: *The History of the World in Six Glasses* by Tom Standage.

Spencer's Legacy: *A Hanging Offense: The Strange Affair of the Warship Somers* by Buckner F. Melton, Jr. *The Chi Psi Story,* edited by George Ray. "A Brief History of the United States Naval Academy" (www.nadn.navy.mil).

Terror from the Skies: *Taking Flight* by Richard P. Hallion. "Bombardment by Means of Balloons." *Scientific American,* March 14, 1849. *Aeronautics in the Union and Confederate Armies* by Frederick Stansburgh Haydon. *The Pocket Book of Aeronautics* by Herman Moedebeck.

The Art of War: *Robert E. Lee* by Emory Thomas. *Whistler, a Life* by Gordon Fleming.

Dressed to Kill . . . or Be Killed: *Fighting Words: From War, Rebellion, and Other Combative Capers* by Christine Ammer. "Why the Charge of the Light Brigade Still Matters," by Sean Coughlan, *BBC News* (http://news.bbc.co.uk/2/hi/uk_news/magazine/3944699.stm).

Over the Hump?: *The U.S. Camel Corps* by Odie B. Faulk. "The Short Unhappy Life of the U.S. Camel Cavalry," by Stanley Kramer, *American History Illustrated,* March 1987. Documents from the consolidated camel file (on microfilm) at the National Archives.

Bite the Bullet: *Gunpowder: Alchemy, Bombards, and Pyrotechnics* by Jack Kelly. *Encyclopedia of Events That Changed the World* by Robert Ingpen and Philip Wilkinson. "*Sepoy Mutiny Echoes Muslim-Western Clash,*" by Andrea Varin, ABC News (http://www.abcnews.com).

Red Cross: *A Memory of Solferino* by J. Henry Dunant. "From the Battle of Solferino to the first Geneva Convention and Beyond" (www.icrc.org).

The Pig War: *The Pig War* by Michael Vouri. "The San Juan Island's 'Pig War,'" by Michael D. Haydock, *American History,* August 1997. "The Pig War," San Juan Island National Historical Park (www.nps.gov/sajh/Pig_War_new.htm).

Native Guards: *The Louisiana Native Guards* by James G. Hollandsworth, Jr. *The Civil War: Fredericksburg to Meridian* by Shelby Foote.

Twenty-four Notes: *Army Letters 1861–1865* by O. W. Norton. *The Army of the Potomac: Mr. Lincoln's Army* by Bruce Catton. "24 Notes That Tap Deep Emotions," by Jari A. Villaneueva (www.westpoint.org/taps/Taps.html).

Three Cigars: *The Civil War: Fort Sumter to Perryville* by Shelby Foote. *The Army of the Potomac: Mr. Lincoln's Army* by Bruce Catton.

Unleaded Zeppelin: *The Eagle Aloft, Two Centuries of the Balloon in America* by Tom Crouch. *Above the Civil War: The Story of Thaddeus Lowe, Balloonist, Inventor, Railway Builder* by Eugene B. Block.

Burial Ground: *Second Only to Grant* by David W. Miler. *Monument of Silence* by Owen Andrew.

A Bitter Harvest: *Come Retribution* by William Tidwell. "Purloined Poisoned Letters," *US News and World Reports,* July 24, 2000. Ulric Dahlgren's miliary service file at the National Archives in Washington D.C. (Here, among other things, can be found Judson Kilpatrick's handwritten letter claiming that he had no knowledge of the alleged orders to burn Richmond and assassinate Davis.)

The Day the Irish Invaded Canada: "Fenian Invasions of Canada," by P.G. Smith, *Military His-*

tory (http://www.thehistorynet.com/mh/blfenianinvasionsofcanada). *The Canadian Encylopedia* (www.thecanadianencyclopedia.com). "The Fenian Fiasco" by A. Welsey Johns, from a collection of essays entitled *Niagara Land: The First 200 Years* (http://ah.bfn.org/h/essays.html).

Chew on This: *Chewing Gum* by Michael Redclift. *Encyclopedia of New York City* by Kenneth T. Jackson. "History of Gum," Cadbury Adams (www.gum-mints.com/history).

Paris Post: *Travels in the Air* by James Glaischer. *The War Animals* by Robert Lubow. *The Pigeon Post into Paris, 1870–1871* by J. D. Hayhurst.

Winds of War: "Typhoons and Hurricanes: The Storm at Apia, Samoa, 15–16 March 1889," Naval Historical Research Center (www.history.navy.mil/faqs/faq102-3.htm). Various articles from the *New York Times,* October 1888–April 1889.

Fighting Joe: *General James Longstreet: The Confederacy's Most Controversial Soldier* by Jeffrey D. Wert. *The Spanish-American War, 1898* by Albert A. Nofi. Various articles from the *New York Times,* May 1898.

A Tale of Two Generals: *American Caesar* by William Manchester.

Glory Deferred: *The Complete Book of the Olympics* by David Wallechinsky. *Patton* by Martin Blumenson.

The Last Charge: "Return to Gettysburg," by James Wensyel, *American History Illustrated,* July–August 1993. *Fiftieth Anniversary of the Battle of Gettysburg: Report of the Pennsylvania Commission.*

Flying Circus: *The Incurable Fillibuster,* by Dean Ivan Lamb. Various news clippings collected by the Air Force Enlisted Heritage Research Institute (http://cepme.maxwell.af.mil/ heritage/info /pdf/lamb.pdf). *Records of U.S. Attorneys and Marshals: Transcripts of Grand Jury Testimony in the Alger Hiss Case,* Harry Truman Presidential Library.

Lights! Camera! War!: *The War, The West, and the Wildnerness* by Ken Brownlow. *The Life and Times of Pancho Villa* by Friedrich Katz. "Villa at the Front: 'Movies' Sign Him Up," *New York Times,* January 7, 1914. "Admits He's a 'Movie' Star," *New York Times,* January 8, 1914.

The Battle of the Luxury Liners: *The Ship That Hunted Itself* by Colin Simpon. Information provided by Cunard Lines.

Christmas Truce: *The War in the Trenches* by Alan Loyd. *Weird History 101* by Richard Stephens. *Silent Night* by Stanley Weintraub.

The Black Swallow of Death: *The Black Swallow of Death* by P. J. Carisella. "Eugene Bullard, Ex-Pilot, Dead. American Flew for French in '18," *New York Times,* October 14, 1961.

One Against War: *Jeanette Rankin, America's Conscience* by Norma Smith. "Ex-Rep Jeannette Rankin Dies," *New York Times*, May 20, 1973. "The Lone Dissenting Voice," by Glen Jeansonne, *American History*, April 1999.

The Female Lawrence of Arabia: *Desert Queen* by Janet Wallach. "The Uncrowned Queen of Iraq," a segment in THE HISTORY CHANNEL® series *The World Before Us*, written and produced by Rick Beyer.

Enigma: *Codebreakers' Victory* by Hervie Haufler. *The Codebreakers* by Simon Singh.

The Good Man of Nanking: *The Rape of Nanking* by Iris Chan. "The Rape of Nanking," written and produced by Jim DeVinney for THE HISTORY CHANNEL® program *This Week in History*, featuring interviews with Iris Chang and Ursala Renhardt.

The Rescuer: *The Odyssey of C. H. Lightoller* by Patrick Stetson. *A Night to Remember* by Walter Lord. "Dunkirk Remembered," a collection of BBC news stories commemorating the sixtieth anniversary (http://news.bbc.co.uk/1/hi/in_depth/uk/2000/dunkirk/default.stm).

The Man Who Saved Buckingham Palace: "Unearthed: Story of the WW2 Pilot Who Saved the Palace," by Anthony Barnes, *London Independent*, May 9, 2004. "Archeologists Dig up World War II Plane," Associated Press, June 1, 2004. "Nazis Crash into London Streets. Crowds Dance and Cheer RAF On," *New York Times*, September 15, 1944.

The Lady Is a Spy: *American Spies and Traitors* by Vincent Buranelli. *Naked at the Feast* by Lynn Haney. *Josephine* by Josephine Baker and Jo Boussion.

Heroes O'Hare: *Capone: The Man and the Era* by Lawrence Bergreen. *Fateful Rendezvous: The Life of Butch O'Hare* by Steve Ewing and John B. Lundstrom.

Gadzooks! "Bob Burns Dead. Radio Comedian," *New York Times*, February 3, 1956. *Stars and Stripes*, March 1, 1918.

An Offer He Couldn't Refuse: *The Luciano Project: Secret Wartime Collaboration of the Mafia and the Navy* by Rodney Campbrell. *Ike's Spies* by Stephen Ambrose. *Strange but True Stories of World War II* by George Sulllivan.

The Youngest Hero: *Dirty Little Secrets of World War II* by James Dunnigan and Albert Nofi. *We Were There, Too!: Young People in U.S. History* by Phillip Hoos. "Man, a Vet at 13, Seeks Discharge," by Dan Frazier, *Fort Worth News and Star Telegram*, April 10, 1977.

The Wright Stuff: *They All Laughed* by Ira Flatow. "Silly Putty," written and produced by Barbara Moran for THE HISTORY CHANNEL® program *This Week in History*.

Pigeon in a Pelican: *Animal Warfare* by Robert Lubow. "Pigeon Pilots," *Progress Thru Research*, vol. 15, no. 1 (1961).

One-Sided Battle: "The Battle for Kiska," by Rhonda Roy, *Espirit de Corps*, vol.9, issues 4 and 5. *Aleutian Islands: The US Army Campaigns of World War II* by George L. MacGarrigle (this brochure from the U.S. Army Center of Military History can be found online at http://www.army.mil/cmhpg/brochures/aleut/aleut.htm). "Janfu," *Time*, August 30, 1943.

A Country of Heroes: *A Conspiracy of Decency: The Rescue of the Danish Jews During World War II* by Emmy E. Werner. "Rescue in Denmark," U.S. Holocaust Memorial Museum (http://www.ushmm.org/outreach/denmark.htm).

The Greatest Hoax in History: *Hoodwinking Hitler: The Normandy Deception* by William B. Breuer. *World War II: The American Story*, edited by Sarah Brash.

Is Paris Burning? *Is Paris Burning?* By Larry Collins and Dominique LaPierre. "Gen. Dietrich von Choltitz Dies. 'Savior of Paris' in '44 was 71," *New York Times*, November 6, 1966.

Patton's Prayer: *War as I Knew It* by George S. Patton, annotated by Colonel Paul D. Harkins. "The True Story of the Patton Prayer," by Msgr. James H. O'Neill, *Review of the News*, October 6, 1971.

Fu-Go: *Japan's World War II Balloon Bomb Attacks on North America* by Robert C. Mikesh. "Balloon Bombs Hit West Coast in War," *New York Times*, May 29, 1947.

Flag Day: *Moments. The Pulitzer Prize Photographs* by Sheryle and John Leekley. *Flags of Our Fathers* by James Bradley with Ron Powers.

Shades of Gray: "Pete Gray" by William C. Kashatus, *American History*, June 1995.

About-Face: *Presidents' Secret Wars* by John Prados. *OSS: The Secret History of America's First Central Intelligence Agency* by Richard Harris Smith.

Floor It: *Ever Green—The Boston Celtics: A History in the Words of Their Players, Coaches, Fans, and Foes, from 1946 to the Present* by Dan Shaughnessy. "Anthony Dinatale, 88. Owned Firm That Built Garden's Parquet Floor," *Boston Globe*, May 7, 1994. Information provided by the Boston Celtics and the Fleet Center.

Bombs Away!: "Broken Arrow: Goldsboro NC" is an excellent, well-documented website (www.ibiblio.org/bomb). "The Story Behind the Pentagon's Broken Arrows: An Arrow Is a Nuclear Weapon. A Broken Arrow is a Nuclear Disaster," by Gary Hanauer, *Mother Jones*, April 1981.

G.I. Joe: *G.I. Joe: The Complete Story of America's Favorite Man of Action* by John Michlig and Don Levine. "G.I. Joe" produced and written by T. J. Winik for THE HISTORY CHANNEL® program *This Week in History*.

Acoustic Kitty: "CIA Recruited Cat to Bug Russians," by Charlotte Edwards, *London Telegraph* (http://portal.telegraph.co.uk). "MI5 Planned to Use Gerbil Spy Catchers," by Richard Norton-Taylor, *Guardian*, June 30, 2001. Information on the chicken-powered nuke from the British National Archives. (The information about this came from a recently declassified secret document. The suggestion has been made that the scientists who originally wrote that document were just trying to see if anyone was paying attention.)

Soccer War: *The Soccer War* by Ryszard Kapuscinksi. " 'The Soccer War' Is Still Not Over," by Richard Severos, *New York Times*, July 2, 1972.

Like Father, Like Son: *Brave Men Gentle Heroes: American Fathers and Sons in World War II and Vietnam* by Michael Takiff. *Dustoff: The Memoir of an Army Aviator* by Mike Novosel, Sr.

Scrap Metal War: *Fight for the Falklands* by John Laffin.

The Domino's Theory: "And Bomb the Anchovies," by Paul Gray, *Time*, August 13, 1990. "The Battle So Far, So Good," by George J. Church, *Time*, January 28, 1991. "Crusty DC Veteran Says War Is Near," *Chicago Tribune*, January 16, 1991. "Pizza: The Year in Review," *Falls Church News*, January 1, 2004.

ACKNOWLEDGMENTS

The mistakes in this book are all mine, but on everything else I had a lot of help.

The *Greatest War Stories Never Told* came into being as an offshoot of the *Timelab 2000*® history minutes that aired on THE HISTORY CHANNEL®. I am eternally grateful to Artie Scheff for asking me to produce the *Timelab* series, and delighted to have another opportunity to acknowledge the team of talented people whose contributions made it a success, especially Alison White, Melanie McLaughlin, Jim Gilmore, Jim Ohm, Patricia Baraza Vos, Jen Pearce, Mike Mavretic, Richard Klug, Megan Reilly, Tom Yaroushek, Rob Stegman, Joel Olicker, Tug Yourgrau, Deb Cutler, Maria Loconte, Patrice Goldman, and Sam Waterston. Their efforts laid the groundwork for these books.

A number of other terrific writers and producers who have worked with me on various documentary projects contributed ideas and material that wound up on these pages. My thanks to Barb Moran, T. J. Winik, Kate Raisz, Jim DeVinney, Jacquie Jones, Julie Rosenberg, Rachel Roessler, and Lena Sheehan. Jacqueline Sheridan, my collaborator on three documentaries (with a fourth in the works), contributed to both this book and its predecessor in ways too numerous to mention. (Let me note that I mistakenly left T.J. and Jacqueline out of the acknowledgments for the first book—guys, I'm trying to make it up here!)

Special thanks to the many other people who took time to suggest story ideas, including Vance Gilbert, Diane Tiraz, the Trotter family, and of course my dad, who remains, at age eighty-five, a font of history nuggets.

Much of the research for this book took place at two great libraries: the Cary Memorial Library in Lexington, Massachusetts, and the Athenaeum in Boston. The librarians at the Cary offered tremendous assistance in tracking down all the far-flung books and articles I requested. The Athenaeum offers an unparalleled collection of nineteenth-century books (among other holdings) and is one of the few places I am aware of where you can check out and bring home books more than 150 years old. I owe a debt of gratitude to both institutions. I would also like to thank the librarians at the National Archives, the Library of Congress, the Naval Historical Research Center, and everywhere else, who assisted in my research efforts.

It takes an army of people to turn a manuscript into a book, so let me thank a few of them here: Gene Mackles, who developed the initial visual concept for the series (and created the illustration of the Acoustic Kitty); Leah Carlson-Stanisic and Judy Stagnitto Abbate, who created the interior design; Renato Stanisic, who laid out the pages; copy editor Ed Cohen (As no man is a hero to his valet, no writer is a hero to his copywriter—thanks, Ed!); Mucca Design, who did another great cover; and senior production editor Mareike Paessler.

I am enthusiastically represented by Arielle Eckstut at the Levine-Greenberg Literary Agency. No one could ask for a better agent than Arielle, who sails through even the heaviest weather with plenty of good cheer and makes everything seem easy.

At HarperCollins, Executive Editor Mauro DiPreta and Associate Editor Joelle Yudin are a great team and take very good care of me. Their patience and guidance are never ending. This is the second book they have ably guided me through, and I hope there will be many more.

My teenage children, Bobbie and Andy, force-fed history for years by their father, have both developed a keen eye for critiquing stories. I have come to give great weight to their comments. Bobbie also worked on some of the photo research, using her fluent French to track down photos her father could not. *Merci!*

My wife, Marilyn, is my comrade-in-arms, my rock, and my anchor. She was the first to read the manuscript in progress, and her comments were, as always, invaluable. This book is dedicated to her because it never could have been written without her love and support. May I someday be able to find words eloquent enough to truly thank her for all she does and all she means to me.

Unless otherwise noted, photo credits for each page are listed top to bottom, and images are listed only the first time they appear. Credits for pages not listed can be found in the credits for the facing page. Every effort has been made to correctly attribute all the materials reproduced in this book. If any errors have been made, we will be happy to correct them in future editions.

Abbreviations
LOC: Library of Congress
NARA: National Archives and Record Administration

Page x: © Bettmann/CORBIS. **Page 1:** Mary Evans Picture Library; LOC (Philip). **Page 2:** © Bettmann/ Corbis; Archimedes Web site by Chris Rorres http://www.math.nyu.edu/~crorres/ Archimedes/contents.html. **Page 3:** © Bettmann/Corbis (top and bottom); Archimedes Web site by Chris Rorres. **Page 4:** LOC. **Page 5:** Author's collection (top and bottom); Photo ArchÈodrome de Bourgogne (CÙte d'Or—France). **Page 6:** Mary Evans Picture Library. **Page 7:** LOC (top two); Mary Evans Picture Library. **Page 8:** © Michael Nicholson/CORBIS. **Page 9:** © Bettmann/Corbis (top and bottom); LOC. **Page 11:** © Bettmann/CORBIS (top and bottom); © Archivo Iconografico, S.A./Corbis. **Page 12:** LOC. **Page 13:** LOC (top and bottom); Leon Weckstein. **Pages 14–15:** University of Newcastle/ Gertrude Bell Project (castle); Mary Evans Picture Library (engravings). **Pages 16–17:** © Bettmann/Corbis (all). **Page 18:** © Bettmann/CORBIS; LOC. **Page 19:** © Bettmann/Corbis (middle); U.S. Naval Historical Center (bottom). **Page 20:** Mary Evans Picture Library; LOC. **Page 21:** By permission of the British Library, Manuscript 47680 (f. 44b)